Cambridge IGCSE® & O Level
Essential
Biology
Workbook

Third Edition

Ron Pickering

Great Clarendon Street, Oxford, OX2 6DP, United Kingdom

Oxford University Press is a department of the University of Oxford. It furthers the University's objective of excellence in research, scholarship, and education by publishing worldwide. Oxford is a registered trade mark of Oxford University Press in the UK and in certain other countries

© Oxford University Press 2021

The moral rights of the authors have been asserted

First published in 2021

All rights reserved. No part of this publication may be reproduced, stored in a retrieval system, or transmitted, in any form or by any means, without the prior permission in writing of Oxford University Press, or as expressly permitted by law, by licence or under terms agreed with the appropriate reprographics rights organization. Enquiries concerning reproduction outside the scope of the above should be sent to the Rights Department, Oxford University Press, at the address above.

You must not circulate this work in any other form and you must impose this same condition on any acquirer

British Library Cataloguing in Publication Data
Data available

978-1-38-200610-1

1 3 5 7 9 10 8 6 4 2

Paper used in the production of this book is a natural, recyclable product made from wood grown in sustainable forests. The manufacturing process conforms to the environmental regulations of the country of origin.

Printed by CPI Group (UK) Ltd, Croydon CR0 4YY

Acknowledgements

®IGCSE is the registered trademark of Cambridge International Examinations.

The publishers would like to thank the following for permissions to use their photographs:

Cover image: Michael & Patricia Fogden/Corbis/Getty Images

p19: Jiri Hera/Shutterstock; p104: Kateryna Kon/123RF; p116: Godong/Alamy Stock Photo; p127: Ron Pickering.

All Artwork by: QBS Learning, APTARA, OUP

Although we have made every effort to trace and contact all copyright holders before publication this has not been possible in all cases. If notified, the publisher will rectify any errors or omissions at the earliest opportunity.

Links to third party websites are provided by Oxford in good faith and for information only. Oxford disclaims any responsibility for the materials contained in any third party website referenced in this work.

When using this workbook you will have the opportunity to develop the knowledge and skills that you need to do well in each of the papers in your IGCSE Biology examination.

The IGCSE syllabus explains that you will be tested in three different ways. These are called Assessment Objectives (AO for short). What these AOs mean to you in the examination is explained below:

Assessment Objective	What the syllabus calls these objectives	What this means in the examination
AO1	Knowledge with understanding	Questions which mainly test your recall (and understanding) of what you have learned. About 50% of the marks in the examination are for AO1.
AO2	Handling information and problem-solving	Using what you have learned in unfamiliar situations. These questions often ask you to examine data in tables or graphs, or to carry out calculations. About 30% of the marks are for AO2.
AO3	Experimental skills and investigations	These are tested on the Practical Paper or the Alternative to Practical (20% of the total marks). However, the skills you develop in practising for these papers may well be valuable in handling questions on the theory papers.

Notice that the **recall** questions (AO1) only account for 50% of the marks – you need to show your skill in using these facts for the remaining 50% of the marks.

This workbook contains many exercises to help you to check your recall and to practise these skills. They will be similar to many of the questions you will actually see in your examination, so you will also be helped to develop the skill of working in an examination. In particular, you will find that many of the exercises cover factual material from different parts of the syllabus – exactly like the more difficult questions in the examination. Each worksheet contains a language lab exercise to help you understand and remember key words. There is also a glossary of important terminology at the end of the book.

The answers to the questions are provided, so that you can assess your own performance. Be honest with yourself when checking the marks – you must not be more generous than an examiner would be! Your teacher will probably be able to help you to compare your performance with the expected standards.

Practice may not make perfect, but it will certainly make better.

Good luck!

Ron Pickering

Contents

Contents

Language lab

True or false?

Respiration is a process in which energy is released by the oxidation of foods.

1. The seven characteristics of living organisms are **respiration, growth, sensitivity, nutrition, excretion, movement,** and **reproduction**.

   Complete this table by choosing words from this list and writing them opposite their correct meanings.

	meaning	characteristic
A	the ability to detect stimuli and make appropriate responses	
B	a set of processes that makes more of the same kind of organism	
C	removal from an organism of toxic materials, the waste products of metabolism, or substances in excess of requirements	
D	a set of chemical reactions that breaks down nutrients to release energy in living cells	

[4]

2. To biologists, classification means

   A giving organisms a name   B identifying organisms

   C putting organisms into groups   D describing organisms

   Underline your answer.   [1]

3. The following is a list of groups that biologists use to classify living organisms

   class   family   genus   kingdom   order   phylum   species

   Rewrite the list in the correct hierarchy of classification.

[3]

Language lab

Fill in the gaps.

In the hierarchy of classification, humans belong to the class ....,

the .... *Homo*, and the .... *sapiens*.

1. The drawings show four common birds that came to feed in an English garden.

| Parus caeruleus | Parus major | Turdus merula | Erithacus rubecula |

a. State which two birds scientists believe are most closely related and explain your answer.

....

.... [2]

b. i. Complete this table showing the external features of these birds. One example column has been completed.

species/feature	all feathers the same colour	dark stripe along length of body	large pale areas on sides of head
Erithacus rubecula	X		
Parus caeruleus	X		
Parus major	X		
Turdus merula	✓		

[3]

ii. Use the information in this table to complete the following key to identify the four birds.

1. No large pale areas on head   go to 2

   Large pale areas on head   go to 3

2. All feathers the same colour   *Turdus merula*

   Feathers of different colours   *Erithacus rubecula*

3. ....

   ....

[6]

Bacteria fit into the classification group called Prokaryotes. Explain the meaning of this name.

1. The diagram shows a single-celled organism called *Euglena gracilis*. This organism has some features which are usually only found in animals and some which are usually found only in plants.

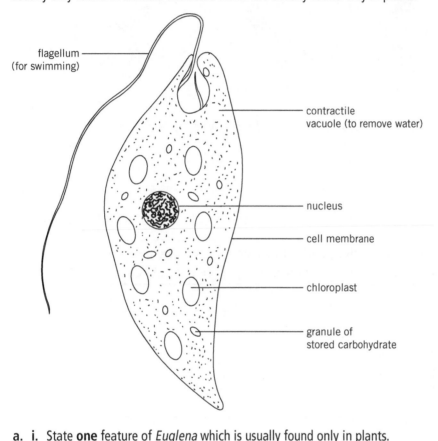

flagellum
(for swimming)

contractile
vacuole (to remove water)

nucleus

cell membrane

chloroplast

granule of
stored carbohydrate

   a. i. State **one** feature of *Euglena* which is usually found only in plants.

.... [1]

       ii. State the characteristic of living organisms which this structure carries out.

.... [1]

   b. i. The contractile vacuole is usually found only in animals. State the characteristic of living organisms carried out by the contractile vacuole.

.... [1]

       ii. The flagellum is more often found in animals. State the characteristic of living organisms carried out by the flagellum.

.... [1]

   c. All living organisms require a supply of energy. State the name of the process which supplies energy to a cell such as *Euglena*.

.... [1]

Fill in the gaps.

All .... have a backbone. There are five .... in this

group, birds, ..., amphibians (none of which have scales), as well as ....,

and .... (which do have scales).

[1]

1. This table compares some features of **chordate** (**vertebrate**) animals.

   a. Define the term chordate (vertebrate).

   .... [1]

   b. Complete this table.

chordate	body covering	constant body temperature	parental care of young
		no	no
	moist skin		no
	scales	no	
	feathers		yes
			yes

[6]

5

True or false?

1. All invertebrates have jointed legs.

2. Spiders and mites are similar types of insect.

3. All insects have three body parts.

4. Centipedes have at least 100 legs.

1. These four animals were among a group of organisms collected from leaf litter lying on the floor of a deciduous woodland.

ant   earthworm   centipede   mite

a. Complete the table below to compare the four animals.

	ant	earthworm	centipede	mite
number of pairs of jointed legs present				
are antennae present? (**yes** or **no**)				

[4]

b. Use this key to place each of the animals in its correct group.

1. jointed legs present	go to question 2
no jointed legs	*Annelid*
2. more than four pairs of legs	go to question 3
four pairs of legs or fewer	go to question 4
3. body in two main parts, legs not all alike	*Crustacean*
body made up of many similar segments, with legs alike one another	*Myriapod*
4. 3 pairs of legs present	*Insect*
4 pairs of legs present	*Arachnid*

Write your answers in the table below.

animal	classification group
ant	
earthworm	
centipede	
mite	

[4]

The following scrambled words refer to plants. Unscramble them.

MEST   AVLEEAS   OLESLULEC   RNESF

1. a. Match up the following parts of a plant with the function performed by each of them.

part of plant
stem
roots
leaves
flowers
fruit

function
absorb water and mineral ions
usually help dispersal of seed, a reproductive structure
hold leaves in the best position
may be attractive to pollinating insects or birds
trap light energy for photosynthesis

[5]

b. Complete the following paragraphs about the lives of plants. Use words from this list – each word may be used once, more than once, or not at all.

algae   angiosperms   autotrophic   cellulose   chlorophyll chloroplast   dicotyledons   ferns   herbivorous monocotyledons   photosynthesis   respiration   starch

All plants contain the light-absorbing pigment called .... This means

that plants are .... – they can make their own food molecules

from simple inorganic sources by the process of .... All the members

of the Plant Kingdom are made of cells surrounded by a cell wall made of ....

The Plant Kingdom includes mosses, ... and seed plants. Many of the seed plants

have the seed enclosed inside a fruit – they are called ...., and exist

in two groups ....(which have leaves with parallel veins) and

......................................(leaves have branched veins).

[9]

The most useful information for producing a dichotomous key is:

- an external structural feature and

- a question which has only two answers (usually YES or NO).

Is this statement true or false?

The diagram below shows four species of marine fish.

A

B

C

D

Use this key to identify the four species of fish.

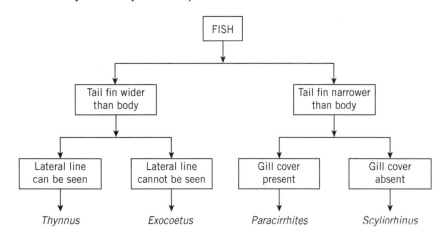

Write your answers in the table:

letter	name of species
A	
B	
C	
D	

[3]

The **size** of a structure or organism is measured in units of **length** (such as mm or m). When a diagram is made, or a photograph taken, it may not be easy to directly show the correct size – for example, when a structure is extremely small or very large.

The correct (or true) size of an organism can be calculated using a combination of actual measurement and a known magnification.

There are two simple relationships that should be understood:

$$\textbf{Magnification} = \frac{\text{measured length}}{\text{actual length}}$$

$$\textbf{Actual (true) length} = \frac{\text{measured length}}{\text{magnification}}$$

It is also important that candidates can use a **scale line** to work out magnification.

|⊢───⊣|
5 mm

> This means that the line drawn represents 5 mm in actual length.

$$\text{So, magnification} = \frac{\text{measured length of scale line}}{\text{actual length of scale line}}$$

$$= \frac{85}{5} = 17$$

Note that there are no units for magnification – it is a comparison of lengths. Be careful to make sure that the two lengths you are comparing are given in the same units.

1. State

    a. How many mm there are in 1 cm ....

    b. How many μm there are in 1 mm...

Core students (Papers 1 and 3) can use millimetres (mm) as units, but candidates taking extension papers (Papers 2 and 4) should also be confident with the use of **micrometres** (μ or μm).

2. The diagram shows a cell from the pancreas of a human.
    The cell was drawn using a light microscope.

    a. Identify the structures labelled **A**, **B**, and **C**.   [3]

    b. Which of these structures would not be present
        in a red blood cell?   [1]

    c. Name two additional structures that you would
        see in a palisade cell from a leaf.   [2]

    d. Use the scale shown alongside the cell to
        calculate how much it has been magnified.
        Show your working.   [3]

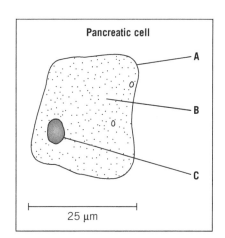

Pancreatic cell

A

B

C

25 μm

Explain why plant cells usually have a fixed, regular shape while animal cells are more flexible.

1. The diagram shows a plant cell and an animal cell.

plant cell

C

animal cell

a. Identify the structures **A** and **B**.

A ....

B ....   [2]

b. i. Use a guideline to join the letter **C** to a possible position of an organelle which carries out aerobic respiration.   [1]

ii. Name this organelle .... [1]

c. State the name of the structure that controls the entry and exit of materials from the plant cell.

.... [1]

d. The animal cell is actually 25 μm in diameter. Use this information to calculate the magnification of the diagram.

Show your working.

[2]

Match the organelles with their functions.

Organelles: **nucleus**   **ribosome**   **mitochondrion**   **cell membrane**

Functions: **protein synthesis**   **active transport**   **respiration**   **site of DNA**

1. a. The diagrams below show a human nerve cell and a palisade cell from a leaf.

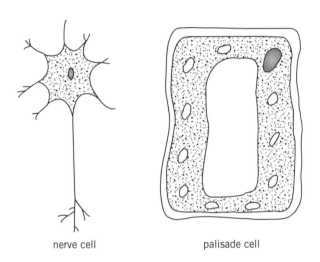

nerve cell   palisade cell

    i. On the diagrams, label **two** features found in both cells.   [2]

    ii. State the name of **one** structure found in the palisade cell which allows it to carry out photosynthesis.

    .... [1]

    iii. State the name of **one** other structure found only in plant cells.

    .... [1]

  b. All living cells are able to release energy by the process of respiration.

    i. State the name of the structures in which aerobic respiration takes place.

    .... [1]

    ii. Energy from respiration may be used in protein synthesis.

    State the name of the structures in which protein synthesis takes place.

    .... [1]

Match the cells with their functions:

Cells: **red blood cell**   **neurone**   **phloem sieve tube**   **root hair cell**

Functions: **sucrose transport**   **impulse conduction**   **ion uptake**   **oxygen transport**

1. The diagrams show several types of plant and animal cells. They are not drawn to the same scale.

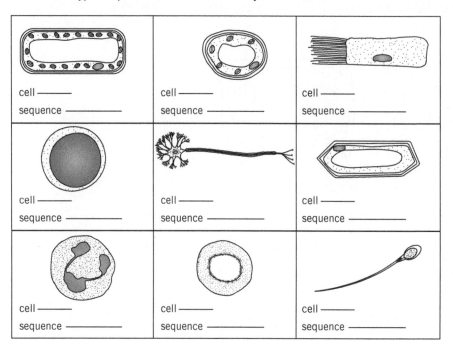

cell ———   cell ———   cell ———
sequence ———   sequence ———   sequence ———

cell ———   cell ———   cell ———
sequence ———   sequence ———   sequence ———

cell ———   cell ———   cell ———
sequence ———   sequence ———   sequence ———

a. Use the key below to identify each of the cells.

Write the letter corresponding to each cell on the line next to the appropriate diagram.

For each of the cells, write down the sequence of numbers from the key that gave you your answer.

Key

1. Cell has clear and obvious cell wall	go to 2	**5.** Cell has projections at one or more ends	go to 6
Cell has membrane but no cell wall	go to 4	Cell does not have projections	go to 8
2. Cell has chloroplasts in the cytoplasm	go to 3	**6.** Cell has projections at both ends	**CELL E**
Cell does not have chloroplasts in the cytoplasm	**CELL A**	Cell with projections or projection at only one end	go to 7
3. Cell with fewer than 10 chloroplasts visible	**CELL B**	**7.** Cell has many projections at one end	**CELL F**
Cell with more than 10 chloroplasts visible	**CELL C**	Cell has a single long projection at one end	**CELL G**
4. Cell contains a nucleus	go to 5	**8.** Cell has nucleus with many lobes	**CELL H**
Cell does not have a nucleus	**CELL D**	Cell has a round nucleus	**CELL I**

[9]

b. Two of the cells that you have identified would be found in the same plant organ.

State the name of this plant organ. .... [1]

Which one of **A**, **B**, **C**, or **D** shows the correct order of structures from the simplest to the most complex?

A organs – systems – tissues

B systems – organs – tisues

C tissues – systems – organs

D tissues – organs – systems

1. Many organisms are made up of cells, tissues, and organs.

    a. The heart, stomach, and bladder are examples of organs found in all mammals.

        State the name of the systems to which each of them belongs.

        Heart ....

        Stomach ....

        Bladder .... [3]

    b. Phloem and stamens are examples of structures found in plants.

        State the name of the systems to which each of them belongs.

        Phloem ....

        Stamens .... [2]

2. When a baby is born it is possible to collect stem cells from the umbilical cord. The stem cells can be stored for many years at very low temperatures.

    a. i. Choose the **best** definition of stem cells.

            A. stem cells are specialised cells and join together to make unspecialised tissues

            B. stem cells are unspecialised cells and divide to make specialised tissues

            C. stem cells are unspecialised cells and join together to make specialised tissues

            D. stem cells are specialised cells that divide and develop into unspecialised tissues [1]

        ii. Doctors believe that they can use the stored stem cells to treat diseases the baby might develop in the future.

            Choose the most likely way doctors might use the stem cells to treat heart disease.

            A. they will produce a medicine for heart disease from the stem cells

            B. they will inject stem cells into the patient's bloodstream

            C. they will make a heart disease vaccine from the stem cells

            D. they will grow heart muscle cells from the stem cells [1]

    b. Umbilical cord blood provides one source of stem cells. Name one other source of stem cells.

        .... [1]

A student gave the following definition of **diffusion**. Is it correct or incorrect? Explain your answer.

"Diffusion is the movement of molecules, down a concentration gradient, across a partially permeable membrane."

1. Complete these paragraphs about the movement of molecules in and out of cells.

   Use words from this list. Each word may be used once, more than once, or not at all.

cellulose	diffusion	down	gas	liquid	osmosis

partially permeable	potential	random	rapid	through	up

   .... is a process in which molecules move ....

   a concentration gradient. The movement may take place in a .... or a liquid, and

   is the result of the .... movement of the molecules. The process continues until an

   .... is reached.

   .... is the .... of water molecules,

   and takes place down a water .... gradient. This process occurs across a

   .... membrane.

   [9]

2.

Movement of materials crossword

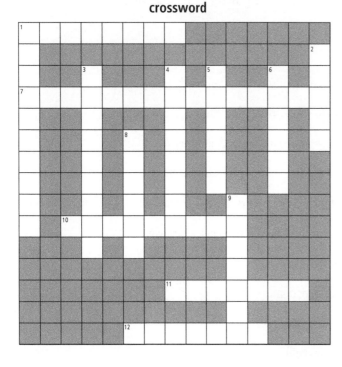

Across:

1　surrounds a cell

7　movement against a concentration gradient using energy

10　see 4 down – the possibility of movement

11　movement of water across a partially permeable membrane

12　protein which can recognise a substance to be transported through 1 across

Down:

1　all of the chemical reactions in a cell

2　with 10 across and 4 down, needed for osmosis

3　movement of particles down a concentration gradient

4　sloping from from high to low

5　required for 7 across – supplied by respiration

6　a substance dissolved in a solvent

8　moves from air sac to the blood by 3 across

9　soluble carbohydrate that moves from gut to blood plasma

[13]

Fill in the gaps to complete this statement about osmosis.

Osmosis is the .... of .... The process occurs across a .... Plant cells which

lose water become .... and plant cells which gain water become ....

1. A group of students carried out an investigation into the effects of sugar solutions on rods of potato. The rods of potato were cut using a cork borer, then gently blotted and weighed.

The rods were placed in groups of three in dishes of distilled water or in one of several sugar solutions of different concentrations. After 4 hours, the rods were removed from the solutions, gently blotted, and reweighed.

The students converted the raw results into percentage change in mass for each sugar concentration. The results are shown in the table below.

concentration of sugar solution (arbitrary units)	percentage change in mass for rod 1	percentage change in mass for rod 2	percentage change in mass for rod 3	mean percentage change in mass
0 (distilled water)	+8	+8	+8	
0.25	+5	+3	+4	
0.5	0	−2	−1	
1.0	−6	−8	−4	
1.5	−9	−10	−11	

a. i. Calculate the mean percentage change in mass for each of the different solutions. Write your answers in the right-hand column of the table. [1]

ii. Plot a line graph of the data on the grid to the right.

iii. From the graph, calculate the concentration of the sugar solution which would result in no change in mass of the potato tuber.

.... arbitrary units [1]

[4]

iv. Suggest the significance of the value you have obtained for part **iii**.

....

.... [1]

b. State the name of the process that causes the change in mass of the potato during the course of the investigation.

.... [1]

15

Use words from this list to fill in the gaps in the following paragraph.

osmosis   haemolysis   turgidity   flaccid   cellulose   starch   active   transport

Water is important in plants for photosynthesis and also to prevent the plants becoming ....

and wilting. Water enters and leaves plant and animal cells by the process of .... Plant cells

can resist the entry of too much water as they have a .... cell wall, but animal cells can suffer

.... (they burst as the excess water breaks the fragile cell membrane).

1. Plant tissues can benefit from cells becoming turgid.

   a. Explain the meaning of the term turgid.

      ....

      .... [1]

   b. Explain how turgor can benefit plant tissue. You should use a diagram in your answer.

                                                                                                                                  [3]

   c. Examine the diagram below. It shows turgid potato tissue placed in a solution.

beaker A   beaker B

10 g weight   potato chip   cork, secured to dish
                                          base by modelling clay

      i. State which beaker contains pure water. .... [1]

      ii. Describe and explain what would happen if the potato chip from beaker **B** was placed in beaker **A** for 24 hours.

         ....

         ....

         .... [2]

Language lab

True or false?

Active transport:

A produces energy

B requires a supply of ions

C requires energy

D moves materials against a concentration gradient

E only occurs in animal cells

1. The diagram shows different ways in which molecules may move in and out of cells. The dots show the concentration of molecules.

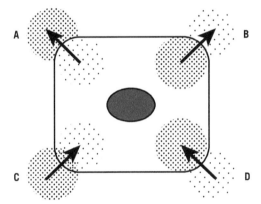

The cell is respiring aerobically.

a. Which arrow represents   i.   the movement of carbon dioxide molecules? .... [1]

                           ii.   the movement of oxygen molecules? .... [1]

b. Which arrow represents the active transport of glucose molecules into the cell? .... [1]

c. Explain your answer to part **b.** ....

....

.... [2]

d. Complete this table to describe **two** other examples of active transport.

example number	name of substance transported	site of transport
1		
2		

[4]

True or false?

All organic molecules contain carbon, hydrogen, and oxygen.

1. Complete these paragraphs about some biological molecules.

   Use words from this list. Each word may be used once, more than once, or not at all.

   **amino acids   cellulose   common   DDT   DNA   fatty acids   glucose   glycerol
   glycogen   haemoglobin   insoluble   simple sugars   soluble   sucrose**

   a. Starch consists of smaller units called .... Another molecule made up of these

   subunits is ...., found in plant cell walls. The sugar most often used for sweetening foods

   is .... which is so useful because it is ....   [4]

   b. Fats are made of smaller units called .... linked to one another by

   .... Fats are often used for energy storage or as barriers between watery environments –

   a property that is useful is that fats are .... in water.   [3]

   c. Proteins such as .... are made of subunits called ....These

   subunits are .... so that they are easily transported from one part of the body to another.   [3]

   d. Nucleic acids such as .... are made of smaller units that act as a code for protein

   synthesis in cells.   [1]

2. Students are able to test for one essential biological molecule using a solution of DCPIP.

   a. i. Name the biological molecule which can be detected with this test .... [1]

   ii. State the colour change which shows a positive result for this molecule from

   .... to .... [1]

   b. The concentration of the essential molecule in a solution can be determined by counting how many drops of the solution are needed to bring about this colour change.

   Look at this list of foods.

   milk   orange juice   strong coffee   fizzy drink (cola)

   Suggest which of these foods contains the highest concentration of the essential molecule.

   .... [1]

Match the following terms in pairs.

| protein | | contain approximately twice as many hydrogen atoms as oxygen atoms |

| fat | | can oxidise DCPIP |

| carbohydrate | | are insoluble in water |

| vitamin C | | enzymes are examples |

1. Soya is a vegetarian meat substitute made from soya beans.

   The table below gives information about the food values of 100 g of soya and 100 g of lamb.

food	energy content / kj	fat content / g	protein content / g	carbohydrate content / g
soya	1800	23.5	40.0	12.5
lamb	1625	21.0	15.0	6.5

   a. i. Use the information in the table to suggest the main advantage of soya compared with lamb.

   .... [1]

   ii. Soya is cheaper to produce than lamb. Suggest one reason why soya is cheaper than lamb.

   .... [1]

   b. The nutrient content of different foods can be investigated with a series of simple chemical tests.

   A group of students was given samples of four different powdered foods. They were also given a sample of pure table salt, which only contains sodium chloride. They carried out three tests, for glucose, starch, and protein. The table shows the colours produced as a result of their tests.

food test	sample **W**	sample **X**	sample **Y**	sample **Z**	table salt
glucose	red/orange	blue	red/orange	blue	blue
starch	brown	blue/black	brown	brown	brown
protein	purple	purple	blue	purple	blue

   i. State which one of the samples contained protein but no starch or glucose. .... [1]

   ii. Suggest why table salt was included in the testing. ....

   .... [1]

   iii. Potato contains starch and protein but not glucose. State which food might have been potato.

   .... [1]

Language lab

True or false?

1. All enzymes are proteins.

2. No enzymes can function under very acidic conditions.

3. Enzymes are only found in animal cells.

1. The two lists show some words referring to enzymes, and definitions of these words.

   Draw lines to match up the terms with their definitions.

word
protein
substrate
product
active site
denaturation
optimum

definition
a molecule that reacts in an enzyme-catalysed reaction
the part of the enzyme where substrate molecules can bind
a change in shape of an enzyme so that its active site cannot bind to the substrate
the ideal value of a factor, such as temperature, for an enzyme to work
the type of molecule that makes up an enzyme
the molecule made in an enzyme-catalysed reaction

[6]

2. This table lists some important uses of enzymes.

name of enzyme	use of enzyme
	part of biological washing powders – removes fatty stains
restriction enzyme	
lactase	
	softens some parts of leather in the clothing industry
	could break down tough plant cell walls
	breaks down starch during germination of seeds

Complete the table by filling in the gaps, using words or phrases from this list.

amylase   cellulase   clears pieces of tissue from fruit juices

   cuts out useful genes from chromosomes   lipase   maltase   pectinase

protease   releases carbon dioxide during respiration   removes milk sugar from milk

[6]

20

Results (or observations) are a record of the measurements made during an experiment. There are certain rules about the way these results should be presented. The results should be recorded in a table, like the one shown below:

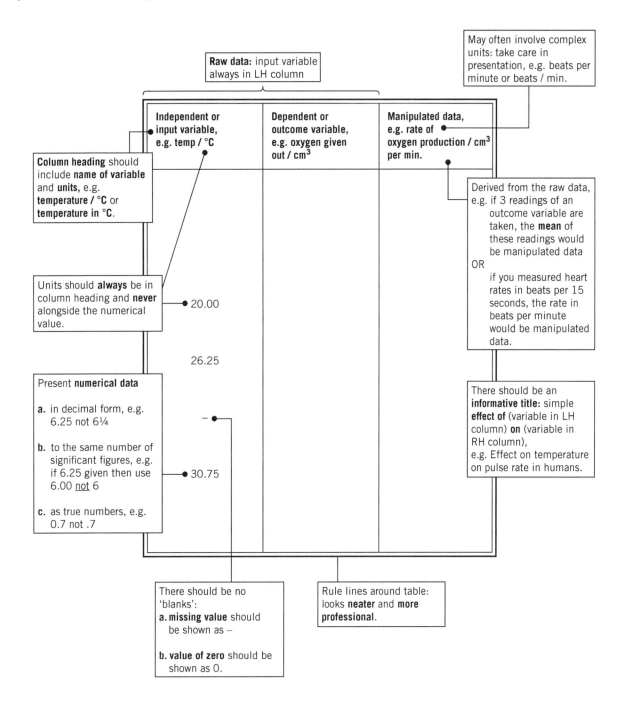

May often involve complex units: take care in presentation, e.g. beats per minute or beats / min.

Raw data: input variable always in LH column

Independent or input variable, e.g. temp / °C	Dependent or outcome variable, e.g. oxygen given out / cm³	Manipulated data, e.g. rate of oxygen production / cm³ per min.
20.00		
26.25		
–		
30.75		

Column heading should include **name of variable** and **units**, e.g. **temperature / °C** or **temperature in °C**.

Units should **always** be in column heading and **never** alongside the numerical value.

Present **numerical data**

a. in decimal form, e.g. 6.25 not 6¼

b. to the same number of significant figures, e.g. if 6.25 given then use 6.00 not 6

c. as true numbers, e.g. 0.7 not .7

Derived from the raw data, e.g. if 3 readings of an outcome variable are taken, the **mean** of these readings would be manipulated data

OR

if you measured heart rates in beats per 15 seconds, the rate in beats per minute would be manipulated data.

There should be an **informative title:** simple **effect of** (variable in LH column) **on** (variable in RH column), e.g. Effect on temperature on pulse rate in humans.

There should be no 'blanks':
a. **missing value** should be shown as –

b. **value of zero** should be shown as 0.

Rule lines around table: looks **neater** and **more professional**.

Sometimes you can see a pattern in your results from the table you have made (see p. 21), but this is not always the case. It often helps to present your results in a different way. **Charts** and **graphs** display your results like pictures and they can make it very easy to see patterns, but only if they are drawn in the correct way. There are rules for drawing graphs and charts, just as there are rules for putting results into tables.

- First of all, look at the variables you measured.

  1. If both of the variables have numbers as their values, you should draw (sometimes we say 'plot') a **line graph**.

  2. If the data can be arranged into groups (sometimes called classes) of equal size then you should draw a histogram.

  3. If one of the variables isn't measured in numbers, you should choose a **bar chart**.

- You should always put the **independent variable** on the **horizontal** (*x*) axis and the **dependent variable** on the **vertical** (*y*) axis. If you don't do this, you can easily mix up the patterns between the two variables.

Several topics in IGCSE Biology can easily be tested by asking the candidate to draw a graph. For example, questions on rate of enzyme activity, population change or change in the mass of tissues in different concentrations of a solute.

The basic rules for plotting a line graph are shown below.

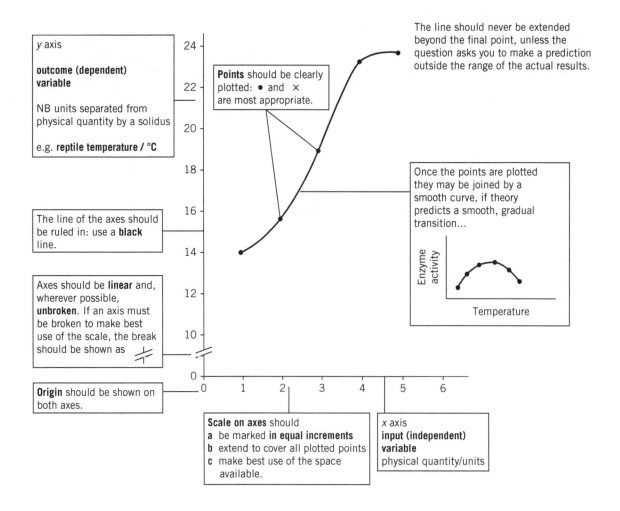

With any graph-drawing question make sure that:

- The axes are drawn the right way round (independent variable on *x* axis (the horizontal axis) and dependent variable on *y* axis (the vertical axis)).

- The axes are labelled. The label should show the variable quantity (rate of enzyme activity, for example) separated from the units by a solidus (a 'forward slash').

- The graph occupies as much of the grid as possible. The grid is usually provided so that the line plotted will occupy most of the space.

- The points have been plotted accurately (as • or as ×). Check carefully any points that don't fit the obvious pattern – you could easily have made a mistake.

- You have not extended the line you have plotted beyond the limits of the results in the table.

- The line has been plotted neatly – a single line with a sharp pencil. The line can usually be drawn from point to point, as it should not change the ability to read another value from the curve.

Making predictions

A graph can let you see a pattern between two variables. For example, as protein in their diet increases, so does the weight of mice. The graph can also let you make predictions if it shows an obvious pattern. So, you might be able to predict how much a mouse would weigh if it were fed on a diet containing a certain amount of protein.

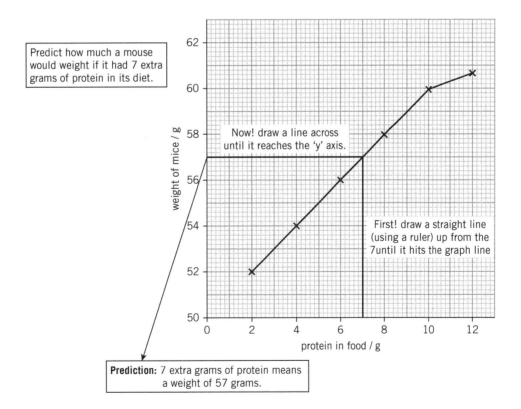

Predict how much a mouse would weight if it had 7 extra grams of protein in its diet.

Now! draw a line across until it reaches the 'y' axis.

First! draw a straight line (using a ruler) up from the 7 until it hits the graph line

Prediction: 7 extra grams of protein means a weight of 57 grams.

Quantitative or qualitative?

It is often easy to see a simple relationship on a graph, but sometimes not so easy to describe it in the best way.

For example, look at this data below. It was obtained from measurements made on the effect of temperature on the uptake of ions by a plant's roots.

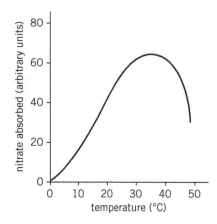

You could be asked to **describe** the results shown in this graph.

A **qualitative** answer would describe this without any numbers. For example, the nitrate absorbed increases up to a peak, then falls away again.

A **quantitative** answer would include numerical information. For example, nitrate uptake increases from 0 to 65 units over a temperature range of 0–35°C. After reaching a peak at 35°C, nitrate uptake rapidly declines to 30 units over the next 10°C.

Which answer provides more information? Which do you think would receive the better mark in an exam?

Of course, many exam questions use the command words describe and explain. If you were asked to do that, you must include some information about the relationship you have described. For example, you might recall that temperature affects the structure of proteins, and that uptake of nitrate depends on active transport which itself depends on protein carriers in root hair cell membranes!

Language lab

True or false?

1. All enzymes are proteins.

2. All catalysts are enzymes.

3. Enzymes are only made in living cells.

1. The rate of activity of amylase is affected by temperature. The effect of temperature was investigated by using a set of six identical test tubes containing 5 cm^3 of starch solution. Each test tube was placed in a water bath at a different temperature and then 1 cm^3 of amylase solution was added to start the reaction.

   The time taken for the starch to disappear was measured. The results are recorded in this table.

temperature / °C	20	25	30	35	40	45
time taken for starch to disappear / s	600	315	210	175	200	420

   a. Use the grid provided to plot a graph of these results.

   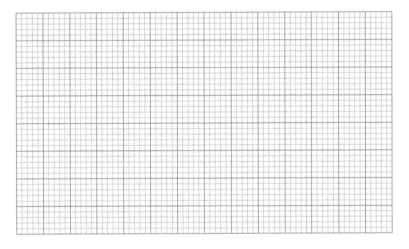

                                                                              [4]

   b. State the temperature at which the amylase works best.

      ....°C [1]

   c. Explain why it is important that the same volume of starch and amylase was present at the start of the experiment.

      ....

      .... [1]

   d. Chemical reactions usually get faster as temperature increases. Suggest a reason why the rate of amylase activity does not increase above 40°C.

      ....

      ....

      .... [2]

   e. Name one other factor that would affect the rate of amylase activity.

      .... [1]

Language lab

Complete the definition.

Denaturation is ....

.... [1]

1. Rennin is an enzyme which causes milk to clot. It is used in cheese-making to start making the solid curd.

   A student decided to carry out an experiment on the effect of temperature on the clotting of milk by rennin. She wrote down her results on a scrap of paper.

   Temp and clotting of milk

   60 – nothing   20 – 35 mins. to clot

   30°c – only 8 mins.   40 – fast – 3 minutes!

   15 – nothing again (no clot)

   55 – 7 min

   45 – fastest yet! – 2 min.

                                   25 – 18 min.

   35°c – 5 minute   50 – 5 min. (same as 35°c!)

   a. Present these results in the form of a suitable table. Draw your table in this space or in your note book.

   [5]

   b. Plot a graph of these results. Use the grid below.

   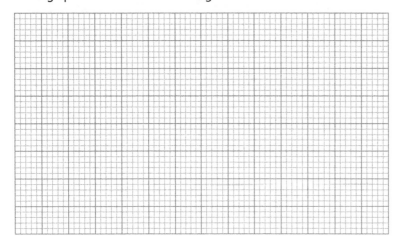

   c. State the optimum temperature for the clotting process ....°C   [1]

   d. i. State one other factor which could affect the activity of the enzyme.

   .... [1]

   ii. Suggest how a student could control this other factor.

   .... [1]

Fill in the gaps to complete this paragraph about enzymes and pH.

Enzymes have an .... pH, the pH at which the enzyme functions most efficiently.

An enzyme which works well at pH 2 could be found in the .... of a mammal, and an

enzyme which works well at pH 8 could be found in the .... of a human.

1. A set of experiments was carried out to investigate the effects of pH on two enzymes, pepsin (a protease) and amylase.

   Each reaction was performed at 37 °C and allowed to carry on for 15 minutes. The rate of activity was calculated by measuring the amount of product formed over the time period of the reaction.

   The results are shown in the graph (right).

   a. i. Name the products produced by the pepsin-controlled reaction.

       .... [1]

       ii. State how much of this product was formed at pH 2.

       .... mg [1]

   b. State the pH at which 60 mg of substance was produced by:

      i. amylase .... ii. pepsin .... [1]

   c. Pepsin works best at low pH (acidic conditions). Explain how these conditions are achieved in the human digestive system.

      ....

      .... [1]

   d. Scientists manufacturing Sparklo, a new biological washing powder, were looking for an enzyme which would remove lipids (fats and oils) from clothes.

      i. Name the enzyme that would remove fats and oils from the clothing.

      .... [1]

      ii. Name the products formed as the enzyme digests fats.

      .... [1]

      iii. Explain how a product of the liver increases the digestion of fats.

      Name of liver product .... [1]

      Explanation of effects on fat digestion ....

      ....

      .... [2]

Complete this word equation by filling in the blanks.

Carbon dioxide + ... = oxygen + ...

1. Complete the following paragraph about plant nutrition.

   The production of food by plants is called .... This process uses

   .... energy trapped by .... in the

   leaves. The process also uses two raw materials from the environment – ....

   from the air and .... from the soil. The first product that can be easily

   detected is .... , a storage carbohydrate. Green plants also produce the

   gas .... during this process – it is released through tiny pores called

   ....   [8]

2. The diagram shows the movement of materials in and out of a leaf during photosynthesis.

   materials in and out of leaf

   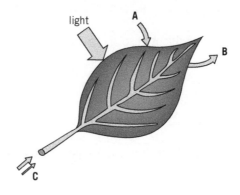

   a. Name the gas entering at **A** ....   [1]

   b. Name the gas entering the atmosphere at **B** ....   [1]

   c. Name the raw material, required for photosynthesis, entering at **C**.

      ....   [1]

   d. Name the mineral, required to manufacture proteins, entering at **C**.

      ....   [1]

   e. State the name of the mineral required for the production of the green pigment in the leaves.

      ....   [1]

Complete this paragraph.

Photosynthesis produces carbohydrates, including the insoluble .... This molecule can be tested for using .... solution, which changes from .... to .... if the insoluble carbohydrate is present.

1. Some plants have variegated leaves (some parts of the leaf are green and other parts are white). A variegated plant was placed in a dark cupboard for 48 hours. When it was removed it had part of one leaf covered with black card and then it was left exposed to bright light.

   After six hours, small discs were cut from the leaf and each was tested for the presence of starch. The experiment is summarised in the diagram below.

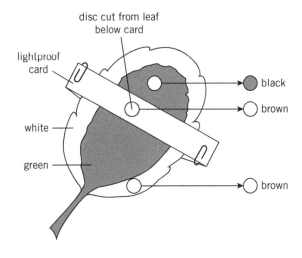

   a. State the reason for placing the plant in a dark cupboard.

   .... [1]

   b. State the name of the mineral required for the production of the green pigment in the leaves.

   .... [1]

   c. Use the results of the experiment to identify one factor necessary for photosynthesis.

   .... [1]

   Explain why this factor is necessary for photosynthesis.

   .... [1]

True or false?

1. Starch gives a deep orange-red colour with Benedict's solution.

2. Oxygen can relight a glowing wooden splint.

1. a. State the name of the main storage compound in plants.

.... [1]

b. Describe how you would carry out a test for this storage compound.

....

....

.... [2]

c. Describe a positive result for this test. .... [1]

d. Suggest two uses, other than storage, for the carbohydrate made by photosynthesis.

....

.... [2]

2. Write a simple word equation for photosynthesis.

[3]

3. Explain why a shortage of magnesium in the soil causes plants to have brown and shrivelled leaves.

....

....

.... [2]

Which one of the following factors is least likely to affect the rate of photosynthesis?

A carbon dioxide concentration

B light intensity

C oxygen concentration

D temperature

1. The diagram below shows a method of measuring the rate of photosynthesis of a water plant such as *Elodea*.

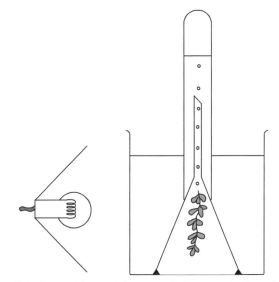

The shoot was exposed to different light intensities and the rate of photosynthesis estimated by counting the number of bubbles released in a fixed amount of time.

The results are shown in this table:

light intensity / arbitrary units	1	2	3	4	5	6	7	8
number of bubbles per minute	6	12	19	25	29	31	31	31

a. Suggest the light intensity at which the plant would have produced 22 bubbles per minute.

.... arbitrary units   [1]

b. Explain how the results illustrate the concept of **limiting factors** in photosynthesis.

....

....

.... [2]

IGCSE calculations sometimes involve **percentages**.

What is a percentage?

Percent means 'out of 100'. The % symbol is a quick way to write a fraction with a denominator (bottom line) of 100. For example, instead of saying 'the sun shone 23 days out of every 100', we say 'it was sunny 23% of the time'.

Percentages can be written as **decimals** by moving the decimal point two places to the left:

$$23\% = \frac{23}{100} = 0.23$$

Decimals can be written as **percentages** by moving the decimal point two places to the right:

$$0.45 = \frac{45}{100} = 45\%$$

Formula for calculating percentages

The formulae for calculating percentages or for converting from percentages are shown below.

To convert a fraction or decimal to a percentage, multiply by 100:

$$\frac{1}{4} \times 100 = \frac{100}{4} = 25\%$$

and

$$0.65 \times 100 = 65\%$$

Examples of percentage calculations

The following two examples show how to calculate percentages.

1. Female earwigs have straight pincers. 12 earwigs out of a sample of 25 had straight pincers. Calculate the percentage of females in the sample.

$$\frac{12}{25} \times 100 = 12 \times \frac{100}{25} = 12 \times 4 = 48\%$$

2. A one-year-old snake was 1.5m long. After one more year's growth, the snake had increased in length by 20%. Calculate the length of the two-year-old snake.

$$1.5 \times \frac{20}{100} = 0.3$$

Thus new length = original length + growth = 1.5 + 0.3 = 1.8 m

Note that in this example you were given units (m). Don't forget to provide them in your answer.

In any calculation it is important to ***show your working***. Even if you make a mistake with your final answer, you will be given credit if you show that used the correct method.

A greenhouse grower may light a paraffin stove in his greenhouse. The most likely reason for this is to:

A remove pest insects

B raise carbon dioxide concentration

C use up excess oxygen

D provide water by condensation

1. A group of scientists working in an experimental plant research station were interested in how different factors play a part in the control of photosynthesis. They made a series of measurements under different conditions. Their results are shown in the table below.

	temperature/°C	light intensity/ arbitrary units	carbon dioxide concentration/%	rate of photosynthesis/ arbitrary units
A	22	5	0.04	80
B	22	10	0.04	80
C	22	5	0.15	170
D	22	10	0.15	200
E	30	5	0.04	80
F	30	10	0.04	80
G	30	5	0.15	185
H	30	10	0.15	300

a. Describe the set of conditions which gave the highest rate of photosynthesis.

.... [1]

b. The normal concentration of carbon dioxide in the atmosphere is about 0.04%. Use the results in the table to describe the benefits of adding carbon dioxide to the air.

....

.... [2]

c. Explain why the rate of photosynthesis is the same in conditions **A**, **B**, **E**, and **F**.

....

.... [2]

1. The diagram shows a section through part of a leaf.

leaf
section

A

B

E

C

0.1 mm

D

a. Name the cells labelled **A**, **B**, **C**, **D**, and **E**.

letter	cell type
A	
B	
C	
D	
E	

[5]

b. State the letter that identifies the cells where most photosynthesis occurs. .... [1]

c. State the letter that identifies the cells which transport water and minerals into the leaf. .... [1]

d. State the name of the carbohydrate that is transported around the plant.

.... [1]

e. Look back at the leaf section. Use the scale to calculate:

   i. the thickness of the leaf

   ii. the length of a palisade cell.

   In each case, show your working.   [4]

State the names of

a. the green pigment in plants

b. the structures in which this pigment is located.

1. The lower surface of many leaves contains pores called stomata. A single stoma is shown on the diagram below.

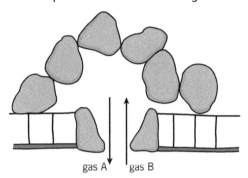

gas A　gas B

a. Gases can move in and out of the leaf through these pores. In the middle of a sunny day **gas A** moves into the leaf and **gas B** moves out.

State the name of **i.** gas A .... **ii.** gas B .... [2]

b. State the name of the process which moves the gases in and out of the leaf

.... [1]

c. Thistles are weeds which can invade fields of crops. Farmers spray weedkillers onto their fields to try to control thistles. One weedkiller is called **This-stroy**.

A group of scientists decided to investigate the effects of **This-stroy** on the thistles. Thistles were grown in two fields. One field was sprayed with **This-stroy** and the other with water. The thistles were left to grow for 10 days, then collected and their dry mass was measured.

The results are shown in this table.

treatment	dry mass of weeds / g					Mean mass / g
This-stroy	20.0	19.1	20.1	19.1	19.2	
Water	33.1	33.3	32.9	32.8	32.9	

i. Calculate the mean mass of the thistles in the two fields. Show your working and write your answers in the table. [2]

ii. Calculate the percentage decrease in the dry mass of thistles when the **This-stroy** is used.

Show your working.

Percentage decrease .... [2]

d. One scientist noted that the thistles had a waxy covering to their leaves. He suggested that this waxy coating could help the plants to conserve water. Explain how a waxy coating can help a plant to conserve water.

....

.... [2]

Language lab

Complete this paragraph about mineral ions by filling in the gaps.

Plants require .... to make the green pigment chlorophyll, and .... to build up

proteins. Minerals can be absorbed against a concentration gradient by the process of ....

1. The diagrams below show the results of an investigation into the mineral requirements of wheat seedlings.

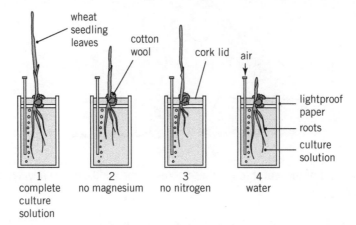

tube number	mineral content	total length of leaves / mm
1	complete	24.5
2	no magnesium	11.5
3	no nitrogen	20.5
4	no minerals	5.5

a. i. Explain why tubes 1 and 4 were included in the investigation.

....

....

.... [2]

ii. Explain why it is necessary to bubble air through the tubes.

....

....

.... [2]

iii. Explain the results for tube number 2.

....

....

.... [2]

b. Farmers often supply these minerals as fertilisers. The bags of fertiliser often have the letters NPK stamped on them.

State what the initials NPK stand for: .... [1]

Most of the energy in our diet comes from:

A vitamin D   **B** protein

C carbohydrates   **D** fats

1. This pie chart shows the proportion of different food molecules in a diet.

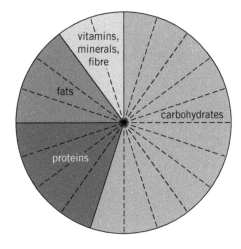

a. Calculate the percentage of the diet made up of carbohydrates and fats together. Show your working.

[2]

b. Choose whether each of the following statements about food and feeding is true or false.

statement	true or false
Starch is a carbohydrate found in bread and pasta	
Meat and fish are essential in the diet, as they are the only sources of protein	
Biuret reagent gives a light purple colour with protein	
Oranges and lemons contain vitamin C, and so may help to prevent rickets	
Fats dissolved in alcohol give a milky white colour when mixed with water	
Bacteria can be engineered to provide proteins useful to humans	
Strawberries are a good source of iron	
Vitamin C can be detected using a blue solution called DCPIP	
Assimilation is the process in which foods are transferred from the gut to the blood	
Starch gives an orange colour with iodine solution	
Calcium helps build strong teeth and bones	
Kwashiorkor is a form of malnutrition caused by a low-iron diet	
Too much fat in the diet causes scurvy	
The most common molecule in the human body is water	
Humans cannot eat fungi	

[15]

If one of the variables in an investigation is not measured in numbers, you should choose a bar chart as a way of presenting the results visually.

This chart displays the results from an experiment in which students were given a choice of one sweet from a selection on a table. Which colour would be their favourite?

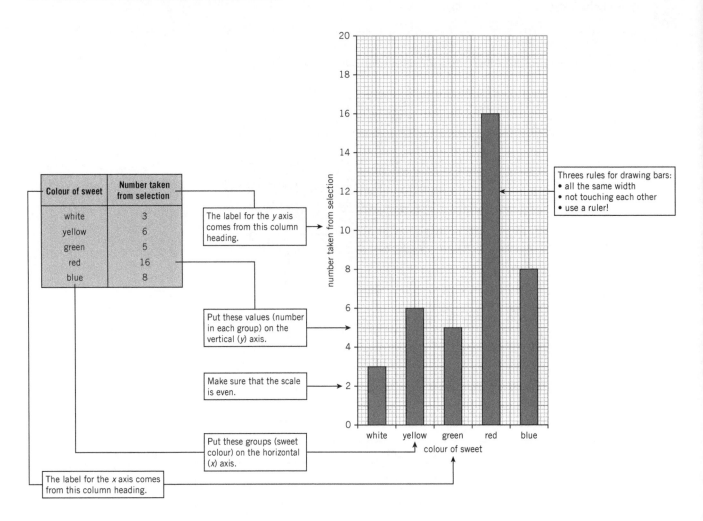

Colour of sweet	Number taken from selection
white	3
yellow	6
green	5
red	16
blue	8

The label for the *y* axis comes from this column heading.

Put these values (number in each group) on the vertical (*y*) axis.

Make sure that the scale is even.

Put these groups (sweet colour) on the horizontal (*x*) axis.

The label for the *x* axis comes from this column heading.

Threes rules for drawing bars:
• all the same width
• not touching each other
• use a ruler!

Language lab

An imbalance between energy needs and energy intake may cause .... and ....

Fill in the gaps from the following choice of words:

obesity   hair loss   diabetes   rickets   scurvy

1. The table below shows the daily energy requirements of different people.

person	energy requirement / kJ per day × 1000
eight-year-old boy or girl	4
teenage girl	12
teenage boy	14
manual worker (builder)	18.5
patient in hospital	7
male IT worker	11.5
female IT worker	9.5
elderly person (aged 75)	8

a. Plot this information as a bar chart. Use the grid provided.

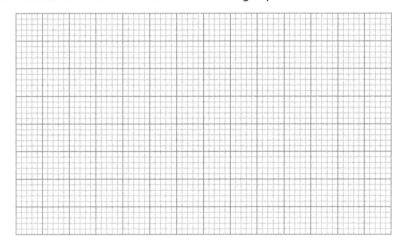

b. Use data from the table to suggest **two** factors which influence an individual's daily energy requirements.

....

.... [2]

c. Suggest why a female IT worker might have a lower energy requirement than a male IT worker.

.... [1]

A deficiency of milk in the diet is most likely to cause ....

Choose your answer from:

diabetes   scurvy   marasmus   rickets

1. The table shows the percentage of overweight people in different age groups in a population.

age group	percentage of overweight people	
	male	female
20–24	22	20
25–29	27	22
30–34	35	27
35–39	40	32
40–44	51	39
45–49	65	44
50–54	64	49
55–59	62	52

a. i. State which sex is more likely to be overweight.

.... [1]

ii. State which group has the smallest percentage of overweight people.

.... [2]

b. i. State the form in which large amounts of extra weight are stored in the human body.

.... [1]

ii. Suggest **three** medical conditions associated with being overweight.

.... [3]

c. Being overweight is one example of malnutrition. Define the term *malnutrition*.

.... [2]

d. A group of doctors studying the growth and development of children noticed that those that did not drink milk often developed weak bones.

i. Name a vitamin present in milk which helps bone growth. .... [1]

ii. Name a mineral present in milk which helps bone growth. .... [1]

iii. Milk is also a source of protein. Suggest why a shortage of protein might be harmful.

.... [1]

1. Human salivary amylase can break down starch. In order to investigate the optimum conditions for starch digestion, four test tubes were set up as shown in the diagram below.

tube A	tube B	tube C	tube D
1% starch solution amylase 37°C	1% starch solution boiled amylase 37°C	1% starch solution amylase 20°C	1% starch solution amylase 37°C hydrochloric acid

a. After ten minutes, samples were taken from each of the tubes and tested separately with iodine solution and with Benedict's reagent.

Complete the table below to show the likely results of this investigation.

	colour in tube A	colour in tube B	colour in tube C	colour in tube D
tested with iodine solution				
tested with Benedict's reagent				

[4]

b. State where amylase is secreted in the human digestive system.

.... [2]

c. Explain why tubes **A**, **B**, and **C** were incubated at 37°C.

.... [1]

d. Suggest where the conditions in tube **D** are likely to occur in the human digestive system.

.... [1]

41

Match the following pairs.

molar		biting
incisor		killing/piercing
canine		crushing

1. This diagram shows a section through a molar tooth.

   a. Name the parts **A**, **B**, and **C**.

      A ....
      B ....
      C ....   [3]

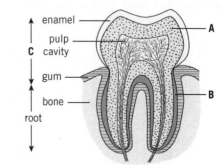

   b. Fibres hold the tooth into its socket in the gum. These fibres loosen
      and teeth may fall out as a symptom of the disease scurvy.

      State the name of the vitamin needed to produce these fibres properly.

      .... [1]

2. The pH of the saliva of 100 students in a school was measured and compared with the number of teeth with fillings.
   The results are presented in the table below.

pH of saliva	percentage of pupils in each pH range	average number of fillings per student in each pH range
6.7–6.9	20	8
7.0–7.2	60	5
7.3–7.5	20	3

   a. Suggest how the pH of the saliva could be measured.

      ....

      .... [2]

   b. State the hypothesis being tested in this investigation.

      .... [1]

   c. State and explain whether the results support the hypothesis.

      ....

      ....

      .... [2]

Fill in the gaps.

In the mouth .... is secreted. This liquid contains the enzyme ....

and the solute .... which makes the pH more ....

1. The diagram shows some stages of ingestion of food.

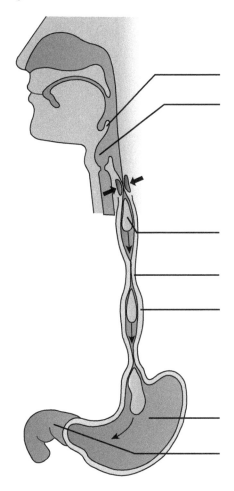

a. Add labels to the diagram, using these words and phrases:

   **bolus of food   circular muscle   contracted circular muscle   epiglottis
   entrance to trachea   relaxed circular muscle   pyloric sphincter   stomach**   [7]

b. List **three** functions of saliva.

   1. ....

   2. ....

   3. .... [3]

The surface area of the small intestine is increased by the presence of:

A cilia   B flagella

C root hairs   D villi

1. Study the structure shown in the diagram (right).

   a. Name this structure. .... [1]

   b. Suggest where this structure would be found.

   .... [1]

0.25 mm

   c. i. Draw a line, labelled M, to show the vessel into which fatty acids and glycerol are absorbed.
   [1]

   ii. Draw a line, labelled N, to show a cell which releases a product to protect the lining of this structure.
   [1]

   d. Describe how this structure is adapted to its function.

   ....

   ....

   ....

   .... [3]

   e. Use the scale line on the diagram to calculate:

   i. the magnification of this diagram

   [2]

   ii. the actual height of the structure, from **X** to **Y**.

   Show your working in each case. [2]

The following words refer to plant transport, but they are scrambled up. Unscramble the words.

LHPEMO   PIEREMISD   MXYLE   CRUOSSE

When you have unscrambled the words, match them with their definitions.

A main carbohydrate transported in plants

B site of water and mineral transport

C outer covering of plant

D tissue which transports sugars

[2]

1. Study the diagrams below.

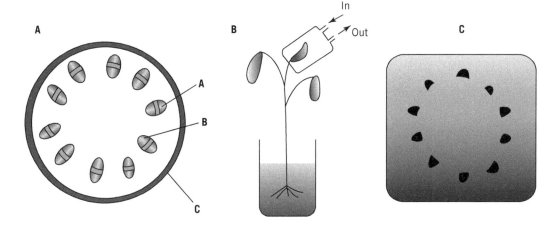

a. Identify the tissues labelled **A**, **B**, and **C** in diagram **A**.

A ....   B ....   C ....   [3]

b. An experiment was carried out using the plant shown in diagram **B**. The roots of the plant were allowed to stand in a solution of eosin (a red dye), and one of the leaves was kept inside a container that could be filled with radioactively labelled carbon dioxide.

The apparatus was placed in bright light for 6 hours. A cross-section of the stem was then cut using a sharp scalpel.

i. State which of the tissues **A**, **B**, or **C** would be stained red. .... [1]

Explain your answer. ....

.... [1]

ii. The section was allowed to stand on a piece of film sensitive to radiation.

When the film was developed it appeared as shown in diagram **C**.

Explain why the film had this appearance. ....

....

.... [2]

Language lab

Fill in the gaps.

Plants need water for .... and as a raw material for .... A plant

takes up water through its .... and loses it through the ....

1. These paragraphs refer to transport systems in plants.

   Use words from this list to complete the paragraphs. You may use each word once, more than once, or not at all.

   **active transport　cambium　diffusion　digestion　epidermis　hairs　ions
   magnesium　nitrate　osmosis　phloem　photosynthesis　respiration
   solvent　support　surface area　transpiration　vascular　xylem**

   Water is obtained by plants from the soil solution. The water enters by the process of ....

   through special structures on the outside of the root called root .... These structures

   increase the .... of the root. As well as absorbing water they can also take up ....

   such as .... which is required for the production of chlorophyll. These substances are absorbed

   both by .... and by .... (a process that requires the supply of energy).

   Plant cells rely on water for ...., as a .... in chemical reactions, and

   as a raw material for .... Water is also used as a transport medium.　　　　[10]

2. Suggest how a scientist could compare the rate of water loss from a thistle and a crop plant.

   ....

   ....

   ....

   ....

   ....

   ....

   ....

   ....

   .... [5]

True or false?

Transpiration causes loss of water and minerals from a plant.

1. The diagram shows the apparatus used by a student in a laboratory
    investigation of the water balance of a green plant. The roots were carefully
    washed before the plant was placed in the measuring cylinder.
    The apparatus containing the plant was weighed at the start of the
    investigation and again 24 hours later. The scale on the measuring cylinder
    was used to read the volume of water. The same investigation was also
    carried out by four other students.

The results of the investigation are shown in the table.

	mass of apparatus / g					mean mass / g	volume of water / cm³					mean volume / cm³
start	220	225	217	221	219		100	100	100	100	100	
24 h later	208	214	209	210	210		87	89	88	87	89	

a. Calculate the mean loss of mass due to water loss from the plant during the 24-hour period.
    Show your working.

    .... [3]

b. Calculate the mean **mass** of water, which has been absorbed by the roots of the plant during the 24-hour period.
    Show your working.

    ....g [3]

c. Using your knowledge of how water moves upwards in a green plant, explain why your answers to **a** and **b** are
    quite similar.

    ....

    ....

    ....

    .... [2]

d. Explain why the mass of water absorbed by the roots is not exactly the same as the amount of water lost by the plant.

    ....

    .... [2]

The contents of the translocation system can be sampled by insects, called ...., which feed on the transported sugars.

1. **a.** The diagrams show transverse sections of a stem (**A**) and a vascular bundle in a leaf (**B**).

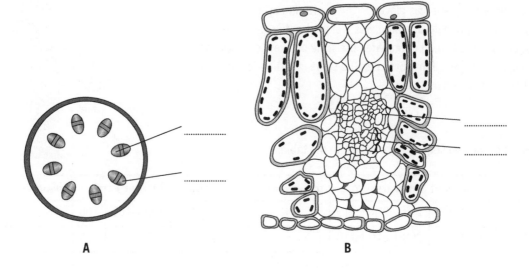

    A   **B**

    On each of the diagrams label the phloem and the xylem.   [4]

   b. The diagram below shows a plant in the sunlight. Three areas of translocation are labelled.

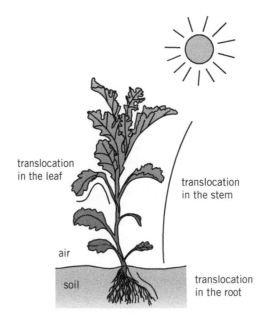

    translocation in the leaf

    translocation in the stem

    air

    soil

    translocation in the root

    i. Add arrowheads to each of the three 'translocation' lines to show the direction of translocation in the three areas.   [3]

    ii. Name the main material which is translocated through the body of the plant.

    .... [1]

Language lab

Match the following pairs.

aorta	from heart to lungs
renal artery	blood input to kidney
hepatic vein	blood output from liver
pulmonary artery	main artery in the body

1. The diagram shows a plan of the mammalian blood system.

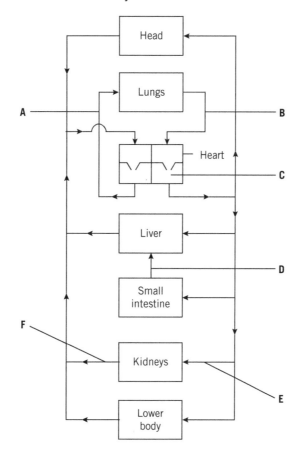

a. i. The name of blood vessel **B** is .... [1]

ii. Suggest **two** ways in which the blood in vessel **A** differs from the blood in vessel **B**.

1. ....

2. .... [2]

b. Suggest **two** ways in which the blood in vessel **E** differs from the blood in vessel **F**.

1. ....

2. .... [2]

c. On the diagram, use a guide line and the letter **P** to show the region where the blood is at its highest pressure. [1]

Language lab

True or false?

1. The semilunar valves are at the exits from the ventricles.

2. The left ventricle has thinner walls than the right ventricle.

1. The diagram shows a human heart that has been cut across in the region of the ventricles.

chamber **X**

chamber **Y**

area **Z**

clot in branch of coronary artery

   a. i. State the name of the chamber labelled **Y**. .... [1]

   ii. Explain your answer.

   ....

   .... [2]

   b. The beating of the heart is controlled by a patch of tissue called a ....

   In a healthy person the heart normally beats at about .... beats per minute.

2. a. In mammals, the blood flows through the heart twice for each complete circuit of the body – this is called a

   .... circulation.   [1]

   In contrast, in fish blood flows through the heart only once for each complete circuit.

   The diagram shows the difference between these two types of circulation.

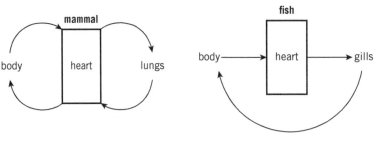

mammal

body   heart   lungs

fish

body ——→ heart ——→ gills

   b. State one **disadvantage** of the single circulation.

   .... [1]

   c. One **advantage** of the double circulation is that pressure is high enough to allow efficient filtration of the blood

   in the paired .... [1]

   d. The veins of fish tend to be much wider than those of mammals.

   Suggest one reason for this. .... [1]

   e. In a mammal, blood is transported to the lungs in the ....

   If pressure in these vessels is too high, ... can leak into the lungs. This
   sometimes happens to climbers at high altitude so that the climbers have difficulty in breathing.   [2]

Language lab

During exercise the heart pumps more blood to the body. To do this there are two changes to the heart's action. Suggest what these two changes are.

1. The graph shows the pressure changes in the left side of the human heart, during one complete beat.

a. Apart from a change in heart rate, how else can an athlete increase the amount of blood pumped per minute?

.... [1]

b. i. From your knowledge of how the heart works, suggest which valves close at points **X** and **Y**. In each case, explain why the valve closes at that point.

....

.... [4]

ii. Where else in the circulatory system are valves found?

.... [1]

iii. What is the purpose of these other valves?

.... [1]

c. Suggest why, If the heart is working poorly, a person may have blue lips.

.... [2]

A doctor usually takes a blood sample for testing from one of a patient's veins. Suggest why the doctor does not take the sample from an artery.

1. The diagram shows changes in blood pressure, speed of blood flow, and the total cross-sectional area of different blood vessels.

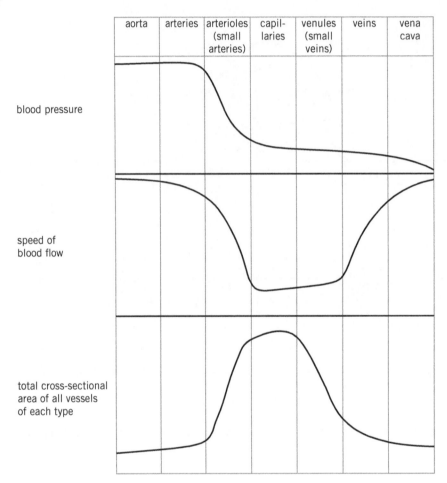

a. i. Name the blood vessel which carries blood at its highest pressure out of the heart.

   .... [1]

   ii. State in which type of blood vessel the blood loses most of its pressure.

   .... [1]

b. i. Name the type of blood vessel where materials are exchanged between the blood and the tissue fluid surrounding the body cells.

   .... [1]

   ii. Use information in the diagram to explain two features of this type of blood vessel which help in the exchange of materials.

   1. ....

   2. .... [2]

Which of the following does not cause problems with the heart and circulation?

A high blood cholesterol

B high blood salt concentration

C low vitamin D concentration

D high protein in the diet

1. a. The table shows the rate of blood flow in cm^3 per minute to organs of the human body, at rest and during exercise.

organ	rate of blood flow / cm^3 per minute	
	rest	exercise
heart	300	400
muscles	1000	4500
gut	1500	1000
kidneys	1100	900
skin	450	1500
brain	800	800
total output	5150	9100

i. State the effect of exercise on the flow of the blood to the organs of the body.

....

....

.... [3]

ii. Explain why the change in blood flow to the muscles is important.

....

.... [2]

b. Regular exercise reduces the risk of heart disease.

i. Explain why a blockage in the coronary artery can lead to a heart attack.

....

.... [2]

ii. State **two** other factors which increase the risk of heart disease.

....

.... [2]

Standard form is a shorthand way of expressing very large or very small numbers and is used in biology as in the other sciences.

There are rules about showing a number in standard form. We say a number is in standard form when it is written like

$$A \times 10^n$$

Where n must be a whole number, and A must be less than 10.

For example,

$$5.4 \times 10^5$$

Remember that $10^5 = 10 \times 10 \times 10 \times 10 \times 10$ so

$$5.4 \times 10^5 = 5.4 \times 10 \times 10 \times 10 \times 10 \times 10$$

To multiply a number by 10 once, move the decimal point one space to the **right**. In this example we must the decimal point 5 spaces to the right (because we are multiplying by 10 five times). It may help to think of 5.4 like 5.40000.

Doing this, we get

$$5.4 \times 10 \times 10 \times 10 \times 10 \times 10 = 540\,000$$

In other words, $540\,000 = 5.4 \times 10^5$ in standard form

Some numbers may be very small, but can still be expressed in standard form.

For example:

$$6.2 \times 10^{-4}$$

This is different because the power is negative, but the principle is the same. Remember that

$$10^{-4} = \frac{1}{10^4}$$

Now, we know $10^4 = 10 \times 10 \times 10 \times 10$.

Having this on the bottom of the fraction means that rather than multiplying by 10 four times, we must *divide* by 10 four times. Dividing by 10 means moving the decimal point to the **left**, so moving it 4 spaces left, we get

$$6.2 \times \frac{1}{10} \times 10 \times 10 \times 10 = 0.00062$$

Therefore, we can see that $6.2 \times 10^{-4} = 0.00062$.

Calculations requiring standard form in IGCSE Biology are most likely to result in large numbers.

For example:

1. A field measures 40 m × 50 m. Students checking the daisy population in the field used 1 m^2 quadrats, and found a mean value of 37 daisy plants per m^2.

    Calculate the total number of daisy plants in the field. Give your answer in standard form. Show your working.

    Area of field = 40 × 50 m^2 = 2000 m^2.

    Total number of daisies = 37 × 2000 = 74 000

    $$= 7.4 \times 10^4$$

2. There are 5 000 000 red blood cells in each mm^3 of blood.

    a. Write this in standard form .... [1]

    There are 1000 mm^3 in 1 cm^3 and there are 1000 cm^3 in 1 dm^3. Humans have 5 dm^3 of blood.

    b. Calculate how many red blood cells are present in the human circulation. Show your working and show your answer in standard form.

    .... [2]

    c. In a human the red blood cells are replaced approximately every 100 days. Calculate how many red blood cells are produced every day in an average human.

    .... [1]

True or false?

1. We have more white blood cells than red blood cells.

2. We need iron to make our blood.

3. We replace our red blood cells every four months.

1. **a.** The diagram (right) shows the composition of human blood.

   i. Calculate the percentage of plasma in the blood.

   .... [1]

   ii. Name two substances transported in the plasma.

   .... [2]

   iii. Match each of these blood cells with its correct function.

cell type
red blood cell
phagocyte
lymphocyte
platelet (cell fragments)

function
engulfing invading microbes
transport of oxygen
part of clotting process
antibody production

[4]

b. The number of red blood cells tends to increase with altitude.

Suggest the symptoms that might be experienced by a climber being flown by helicopter directly, without training, to 3000 m.

....

.... [2]

c. Athletes who compete in races over distances from 1500 to 10 000 m do better if they live or train at altitudes greater than 2500 m.

Suggest a reason for their improved performance.

.... [1]

d. Some racing cyclists have used the drug EPO to increase the number of red blood cells they have.

State the name of one other drug which has been used to 'cheat' in sport. Explain the biological reason for an athlete using this drug.

Drug ....

Reason for use .... [2]

55

Language lab

An organism which causes disease is:

A   a bacterium

B   a fungus

C   a predator

D   a pathogen

1   a.   State **one** symptom of a person suffering from food poisoning.

.... [1]

    b.   Describe how a mother could spread food poisoning bacteria to her child.

....

....

.... [3]

    c.   Suggest **one** way a mother could make sure that she did not spread bacteria to her child.

.... [1]

2.   Not all diseases are spread from person to person. These diseases are **non-transmissible diseases**.

    Non-transmissible diseases may be caused by a number of factors.

    Suggest **one** disease which may be caused by **each** of the following factors.

    Deficiency in diet .... [1]

    Inheritance .... [1]

    Age-related degeneration .... [1]

    Lifestyle .... [1]

3.   Disease-causing organisms *may* be spread from person to person.

    Suggest three ways (apart from in contaminated food) that this could happen.

....

....

.... [3]

Which of the following is not a function of white blood cells?

A production of antibodies   **B** clotting of blood

C engulfing bacteria   **D** recognising viruses

1. Match the following words to their definitions.

word		definition
pathogen		external barriers to infection
transmissible disease		defence against a pathogen by antibody production in the body
antigen		white blood cell which engulfs pathogens
skin and nasal hairs		short term defence by provision of antibodies from another individual
active immunity		a disease-causing organism
passive immunity		a substance which triggers the immune response
phagocyte		cell which produces antibodies
lymphocyte		condition in which the pathogen can be passed from one host to another

[8]

2. This graph shows the level of antibody in the blood in response to two doses of a vaccine.

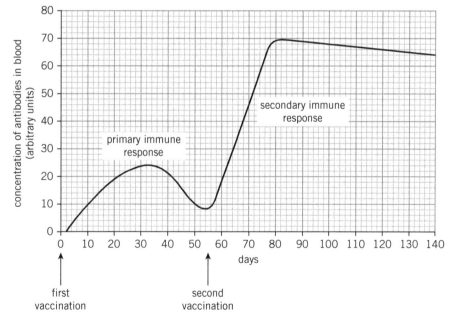

a. Define the term **vaccine**. ....

....

.... [2]

b. State **two** ways in which the response to the second injection is different to the response to the first injection.

....

.... [2]

Complete this sentence.

A second infection by a pathogen brings about a faster response because of the presence of

.... cells.

1. The diagram below shows an action taken by one group of blood cells against infection by a pathogen.

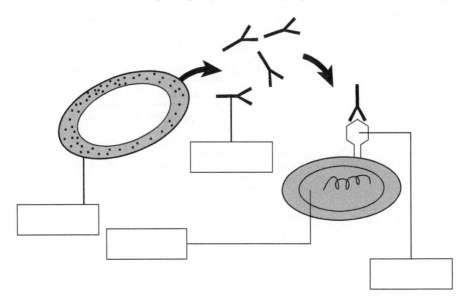

   a. Complete the diagram using words from the following list:

   antibody   antigen   antibiotic   leucocyte   lymphocyte   pathogen

   [4]

   b. Suggest **two** ways in which the invading pathogen may be destroyed.

   1. ....

   ....

   2. ....

   .... [2]

   c. Doctors can protect the body by providing molecules which stimulate the immune response.

   Name this process of protection.

   .... [1]

Immunity can safely result from injection of:

A a pathogen

B a vaccine

C an antibiotic

D blood serum

1. A vaccine has been developed against the organism that causes TB (tuberculosis). The vaccine has been available for use in many parts of Africa from late in the 20th century.

   a. Vaccination against TB is an example of **active immunity**.

      Define the term active immunity.

      ....

      ....

      .... [2]

   b. State **three** ways in which **passive immunity** differs from active immunity.

      ....

      ....

      .... [3]

   c. Complete the table below to show whether each method is active or passive.

method of gaining immunity	type of immunity (active or passive)
vaccination against meningitis	
antibodies cross the placenta and enter the fetus	
a person bitten by a dog is given a serum	
a baby feeds on colostrum (first milk)	
a person becomes infected with a pathogen	

2. Scientists have developed vaccines which can provide protection against COVID-19. Some of these vaccines use an attenuated (inactivated) virus particle to carry the COVID-19 genetic material into the person to be protected.

   a. State the name given to this type inactivated virus.

      .... [1]

   b. Explain why this virus must be inactivated.

      .... [1]

A bacterial infection can be controlled with:

A an antibiotic

B an antiseptic

C a disinfectant

D an antidote

1. The pie chart shows the number of food poisoning incidents reported from different food sources.

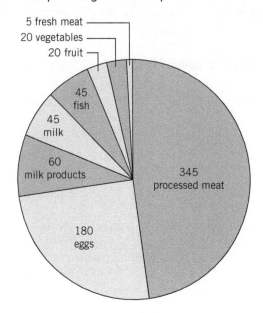

5 fresh meat
20 vegetables
20 fruit
45 fish
45 milk
60 milk products
345 processed meat
180 eggs

   a. Complete this table using the information in the pie chart.

food source	number of reported outbreaks
eggs	180
	45
fruit	
milk	
	60
processed meat	345
	20

[3]

   b. Packaging on products such as processed meat usually includes the instruction 'keep refrigerated'.

   Explain why refrigeration makes processed food less likely to cause food poisoning.

   ....

   .... [2]

Complete the following sentence.

The large intestine can be divided – in the correct order – into the ...., the

...., and the ....

1. The diagram below shows the large intestine of a human.

  a. Use guidelines and labels to identify:

    i. a region in which water is reabsorbed

    ii. a region in which faeces are stored

    iii. the appendix.   [6]

  b. The large intestine may become infected by a bacterium.

    i. Name one disease of the large intestine caused by a bacterium.

    .... [1]

    ii. Describe and explain one symptom of this disease.

    ....

    ....

    .... [2]

  c. Explain why a supply of clean water helps to prevent the spread of this disease.

    ....

    ....

    .... [2]

61

Fill in the gaps.

As air leaves the lungs during exhalation, it passes through the ....,

the ...., and the .... before entering the mouth and moving

into the atmosphere.

1. The diagram shows a section through the thorax (chest).

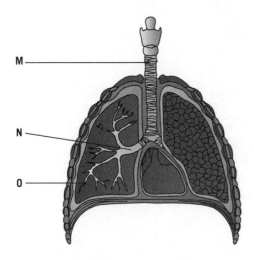

a. Name the structures labelled **M**, **N**, and **O**.

   M ....

   N ....

   O ....   [3]

b. On the diagram, use labels and guidelines to identify two different muscles.   [4]

c. When muscles contract, they use energy supplied by respiration.

   Give **two** other different ways in which this energy may be used.

   1. ....

   2. .... [2]

d. Exhaled air differs from inhaled air. Name **two** gases which are present in higher concentration in exhaled air.

   1. ....

   2. .... [2]

Fill in the gaps.

Oxygen enters the blood at the .... – it crosses the walls by the process of

.... At the same time, the gas .... leaves the blood.

1. This diagram shows an alveolus (airsac) and a blood capillary.

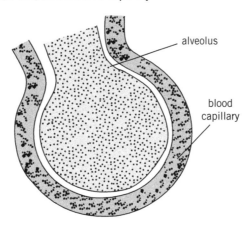

alveolus

blood
capillary

a. On the diagram, use arrows and suitable labels to describe the movement of oxygen and carbon dioxide during gas exchange. [2]

b. List **three** features which make alveoli adapted to gas exchange.

   1. ....

   2. ....

   3. .... [3]

c. State the name of the artery that brings deoxygenated blood to the capillary.

   .... [1]

2. a. State the name of one disease which affects gas exchange in humans.

   .... [1]

   b. Explain why this disease reduces the rate of gas exchange.

   .... [2]

3. Gas exchange is necessary for aerobic respiration to occur.

   Write out a word equation for aerobic respiration.

   .... [2]

True or false?

1. Exhalation uses more energy than inhalation.

2. Breathing releases energy from food.

1. The diagram shows the position and shape of the human thorax (chest) during inhalation (breathing in).

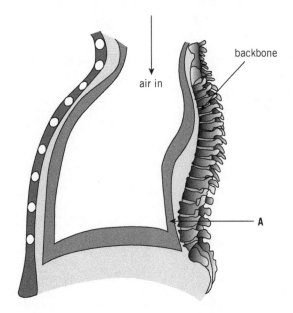

air in

backbone

A

a. State the name of the part labelled **A**.

.... [1]

b. On the diagram label the diaphragm. Use a guideline and the letter **D**. [1]

c. The diaphragm contains muscles involved in breathing. Name another set of muscles involved in breathing in.

.... [1]

d. Describe and explain the how muscles are involved in exhalation (breathing out).

....

....

....

....

.... [3]

Language lab

A young athlete took 20 breaths per minute – the volume of each breath was 2000 cm³. At each breath 20% of the inspired air was oxygen and 16% of the expired air was oxygen. The volume of oxygen absorbed per minute was:

A 40 cm³

B 1600 cm³

C 4000 cm³

D 16 000 cm³

1. A student breathed into a special 'breathing bag' five times. The bag was empty at the start of the measurement.

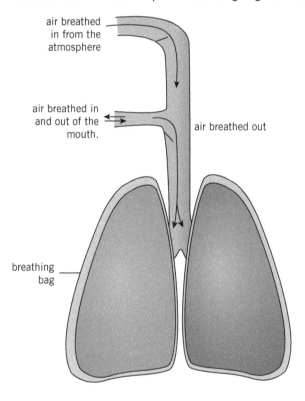

air breathed
in from the
atmosphere

air breathed in
and out of the
mouth.

air breathed out

breathing
bag

a. After breathing out five times the volume of air in the bag was measured. The volume was 2500 cm³.

The student then carried out some exercise for three minutes, and the volume in the bag was measured. This time there was 8000 cm³ of air.

Use this information to describe the effect of exercise on breathing. ....

....

.... [2]

b. The rate of breathing is controlled by the concentration of a gas which increases during exercise.

   i. Name this gas. .... [1]

   ii. Name the process which removes this gas from the blood. .... [1]

1. This piece of apparatus is used to study gas exchange.

glass tube   tomato fruits   capillary tube   scale (cm)

initial position of marker
(drop of coloured liquid)

soda lime to absorb   gauze
carbon dioxide   platform

   a. During the course of the experiment the marker moves.

      i. State the name of the process, carried out by the cells of the tomatoes, which causes this movement.

         .... [1]

      ii. State the direction in which the marker will move. .... [1]

      iii. Explain your answer to part ii. ....

         .... [1]

      iv. Calculate the position of the centre of the marker after 40 minutes, if the marker moves 0.25 cm every five
          minutes. Show your working.

                                                                                                                              [2]

      v. Suggest a suitable control for this experiment.

         ....

         .... [1]

   b. The class teacher told the students that fruit growers often enclosed the fruits they collect in plastic bags filled
       with nitrogen gas.

       Explain why this is important.

       ....

       ....

       .... [2]

1. A group of students wanted to compare the rate of respiration in four different fruits, as well as in tomatoes.

    a. For this experiment, state the **independent variable** and the **dependent variable**, and suggest one variable that should be **fixed**.

Independent variable	Dependent variable	Fixed variable

[3]

    b. This table contains their results.

Tomato	1.55	1.50	1.45	1.50
Damson	0.75	0.75	0.75	0.75
Apple	1.00	1.05	0.95	1.00
Strawberry	1.26	1.20	1.23	1.23
Blackberry	0.90	0.90	0.90	0.90

The students forgot to provide headings for the columns in their table.

Suggest suitable column headings and write them into the spaces at the head of each column.

[4]

    c. Use the grid below to plot a bar chart of their results.

[4]

A pie chart (or a circle chart) is a circle, which is divided into slices to illustrate numerical proportion. In a pie chart, the central angle of each slice is proportional to the quantity it represents.

Pie charts help people to see data in a very visual way, although most scientists prefer to use a bar chart to do this. In an exam, you might be asked to complete a pie chart – you would usually be given the outline of a circle with the quadrants drawn in for you.

An example is shown below.

As with graphs, bar charts and histograms, there are certain rules to stick to if you are plotting a pie chart.

- The sectors should be in rank order, with the largest first

- The first sector should begin at 'noon', i.e. at the top of the chart

- Ideally there should not be more than a total of six sectors

Invertebrates collected in a forest

insects	55%
spiders	20%
snails	12%
worms	8%
centipedes	5%

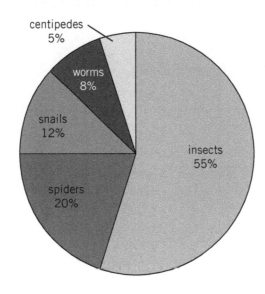

1. During exercise muscle contraction requires energy. Some of this energy is released during aerobic respiration.

   a. i. Write a chemical equation for aerobic respiration.

                                                                                      [3]

      ii. Suggest why respiration is affected by temperature.

      .... [1]

   b. If the muscles work very hard the cells may use up all of the available oxygen. If this happens, energy can still be released by anaerobic respiration. These pie charts show the relative amounts of aerobic and anaerobic respiration during a 100 m race and during a 1500 m race.

pie chart **A**   pie chart **B**

key
aerobic respiration
anaerobic respiration

      i. State and explain which of the pie charts shows the results from a 1500 m race.

      ....

      ....

      .... [2]

      ii. State the effect of a build-up of lactic acid on an athlete's performance.

      ....

      .... [2]

      iii. Explain how the level of lactic acid in the blood is reduced after a race.

      ....

      ....

      .... [2]

   c. Explain what is meant by an **oxygen debt**.

      ....

      .... [2]

Removal of the waste products of metabolism is called:

A egestion

B deamination

C defecation

D excretion

1. a. Define the term **excretion**. ....

.... [2]

b. Complete this table about human excretory products.

name of excretory product	site of production	process responsible for product	site of removal of product
carbon dioxide			
		deamination	
sodium chloride		excess in diet	

[3]

c. The diagram below shows some of the organs in the abdomen, and the blood vessels which supply them.

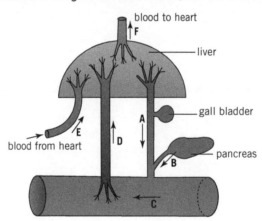

i. State one important function of the liver. ....

.... [1]

ii. Look at the table below. Use guidelines to link each letter with the name of the appropriate structure and a statement about its contents.

letter
A
B
C
D
E
F

structure
hepatic artery
small intestine
bile duct
hepatic portal vein
pancreatic duct
hepatic vein

contents
food
enzymes including amylase and protease
dissolved foods
bile
oxygenated blood
deoxygenated blood

Which one of the following systems includes the kidneys?

A   circulatory

B   digestive

C   reproductive

D   excretory

1. The diagram shows part of the structure of a kidney, and a single cell from region **A**.

a. Name the vessel supplying blood at **X**. .... [1]

b. Name the ball of capillaries shown in the diagram. .... [1]

c. Explain why glucose can cross the wall at **A** but red blood cells cannot.

    .... [1]

d. Suggest **two** features of the single cell from region **A** which are adaptations to its function.

    1. ....

    2. .... [2]

e. The action of the kidney is to produce urine. Name the tube which carries urine away from the kidney.

    .... [1]

True or false?

Urea is produced in the liver and removed via the kidneys.

1. Three test tubes were set up as shown in the diagram below.

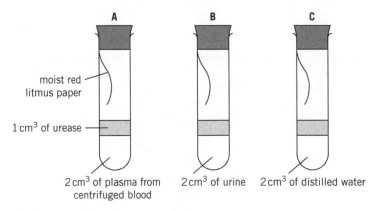

moist red
litmus paper

1 cm³ of urease

2 cm³ of plasma from   2 cm³ of urine   2 cm³ of distilled water
centrifuged blood

The enzyme urease breaks down urea to release ammonia.

$$urea \longrightarrow carbon\ dioxide + ammonia$$

The tubes were incubated at 37°C for 30 minutes. After 30 minutes the contents of the tubes are subjected to several tests. The results are shown below.

	A	B	C
test substance			
biuret reagent	blue to violet	remains blue	remains blue
Benedict's reagent	blue to orange-red on heating	no change on heating	no change on heating
moist red litmus paper	turns blue	turns blue	no change

a. State the name of the substance which the tests show is present in the plasma and in the urine.

.... [1]

b. Explain why the test tubes were incubated at 37°C.

....

.... [2]

c. i. Identify which substances are found in blood plasma but not in urine or distilled water.

.... [2]

ii. Explain why these substances are not lost from the body.

....

.... [2]

d. State the function of tube **C**.

.... [1]

Fill in the gaps. [5]

The material which covers an axon is called ...., and it acts as an electrical

.... during the conduction of an ....

1. This diagram shows a single neurone.

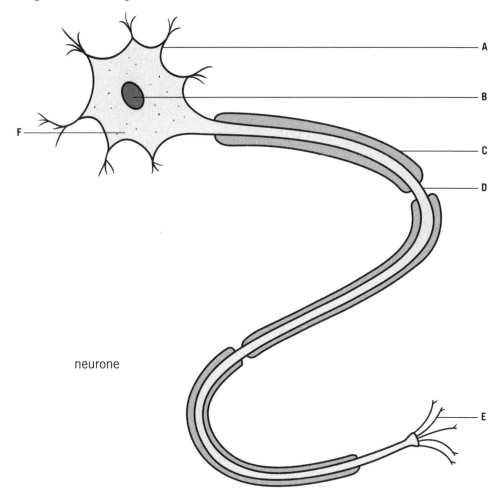

neurone

Match the letters to the descriptions of each of these parts.

description of part	letter corresponding to part
connects with another neurone	
insulates the neurone to prevent interference with other neurones	
contains high concentrations of neurotransmitters	
connects with an effector, such as a muscle	
allows an impulse to 'jump' quickly along the axon	
contains DNA	

[5]

Language lab

Coughing, sneezing, and blinking are all examples of reflexes. Suggest **two** features which all reflexes show.

1. a. i. Sneezing is a reflex action. Name the organ containing the receptor cells which detect the stimulus that leads to sneezing.

[1]

ii. Suggest **one** advantage of reflex actions.

....

.... [1]

b. i. The diagram below shows a reflex arc.

Select words from this list to name the parts numbered 1–7.

**association neurone   dorsal root   grey matter   motor neurone
receptor   sensory neurone   spinal cord   synapse   ventral root
white matter**

structure	name of structure
1	
2	
3	
4	
5	
6	
7	

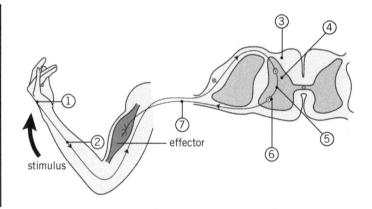

[7]

ii. Muscles and glands are effector organs. State how muscles and glands react when they are stimulated.

Muscles ....

Glands ....   [2]

Fill in the gaps.

A nerve cell is also known as a .... Impulses enter the cell body through the

.... and leave the cell body along an ....

1. The diagram below shows a single synapse.

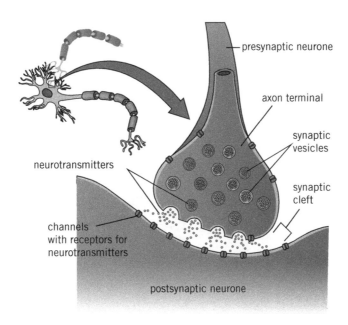

presynaptic neurone

axon terminal

synaptic vesicles

neurotransmitters

synaptic cleft

channels with receptors for neurotransmitters

postsynaptic neurone

a. Use the diagram to define:

   i. Neurotransmitter ....

   .... [1]

   ii. Synapse ....

   .... [1]

b. Explain how a synapse is important in the operation of a reflex arc.

   ....

   .... [2]

A change in the environment which causes a reaction in a receptor is a:

A synapse

B stimulus

C mutation

D synthesis

1. The diagram shows a tennis player. The player uses different receptors during a tennis match.

a. Complete this table to describe the function of these receptors.

letter	name of receptor/sense organ	function of receptor
A		
B	nose	
C		
D		detects position – important in balance

[6]

b. All receptors convert a stimulus into a 'message'. State the nature of this message, and briefly explain how the messages reach the central nervous system.

....

....

.... [2]

Which of the following is **not** a part of the mammalian eye?

A retina

B rectum

C rod

D choroid

1. The diagram shows a section through the eye.

   a. Use the table below to match up the lettered structures with the descriptions of their functions.

description	letter
contains rods and cones	
helps to converge light towards the retina	
is black to prevent internal reflection of light	
is tough enough to act as an attachment for the muscles that move the eye in its socket	
is a muscle controlling the amount of light entering the eye	
contains neurones leading to the visual centre in the brain	

[6]

   b. The diagram also shows the pathway of an important reflex involved in protection of the eye.

      i. Complete and rearrange the boxes to show that you understand the pathway of this action.

      receptor is ....

      effector is ....

      stimulus is ....

      response is ....

      coordinator is ....

[6]

      ii. State the survival value of this reflex.

      .... [1]

Language lab

Which one of the following organs produces both digestive enzymes and hormones?

A adrenal gland   B ovary

C pancreas   D pituitary

1. a. Define the terms.

Hormone ....

.... [1]

Target organ ....

.... [1]

b. State **two** ways in which control by hormones is different from control by the nervous system.

1. ....

....

2. ....

.... [2]

2.

Hormones crossword

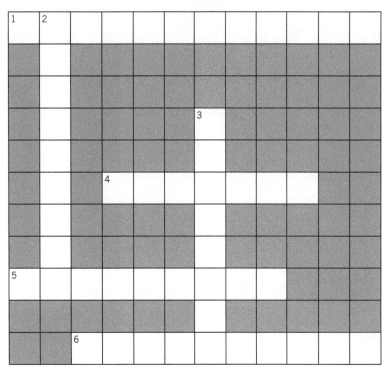

Across:
1 the male sex hormone
4 lowers blood glucose concentration
5 a hormone is a chemical ....
6 responsible for the fight or flight response

Down:
2 internally secreting
3 action balances 4 across and raises blood glucose concentration

[6]

Fill in the gaps.

.... is the set of processes which keep constant conditions in the body.

This set of processes usually rely on .... feedback.

A medical student volunteer agreed to eat a sugary meal then to give a blood sample every hour for the next 12 hours.

The blood samples were analysed for the presence of glucose.

The results are presented in this table.

	Time of day / hours	Blood sugar level / mg glucose per 100 cm³ of blood
Meal taken	06.45	80
	07.00	80
	07.30	90
Point **A**	08.00	128
	09.00	120
	10.00	109
	11.00	100
Snack meal taken	12.00	92
	13.00	105
Point **B**	14.00	120
	15.00	94
Point **C**	16.00	100
	17.00	88
	18.00	84
	19.00	92

a. Present these results as a line graph. Use the grid provided.

[4]

b. Explain why the blood glucose concentration does not rise immediately after the meal.

....

.... [1]

c. i. Explain why the blood glucose levels fall at points **A**, **B** and **C**.

....

....

....

.... [2]

ii. Use these results to define the term **negative feedback**.

....

....

....

.... [2]

d. Draw a second line on the graph (use a different colour of pencil or pen) to show the results which might have been expected for a person with Type 1 Diabetes. [2]

e. Blood glucose levels increase sharply following a fright or shock.

i. Explain why this happens.

....

....

.... [2]

ii. Suggest **two** other changes which could occur in the functioning of the body because of the fright.

1. ....

....

2. ....

.... [2]

Which of the following would not result from a rise in body temperature?

A shivering   **B** vasodilation

C sweating   **D** lowering hairs on the skin

[ ]

1. The diagram shows a section through human skin.

a. State the name of the parts labelled **A**, **B**, and **C**.

A ....   B ....   C .... [3]

b. State and explain the function of the fat cells.

....

....

.... [2]

c. The body temperature of a mammal remains constant within narrow limits in spite of changes in the environmental temperature.

State **two** ways in which this 'constant' body temperature is valuable to mammals.

1. ....

....

2. ....

.... [2]

The following words are scrambled versions of terms associated with plant responses. Unscramble the words.

XAUNI   TOIMSVGRAIPR   TMIOSHPTOORP

Auxin is a hormone made by the tips of plant shoots.

1. **a.** A shoot was grown in a container so that light shone onto it from one side only. This set of diagrams shows movement of the auxin in the shoot, and the results of the experiment.

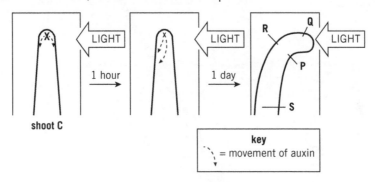

i. Describe the movement of auxin in the shoot after one hour.

.... [1]

ii. Use the diagram to explain how the movement of auxin causes the plant response seen in this investigation.

....

....

....

.... [2]

iii. Name the plant response seen above, and explain its value to a plant.

Name of response .... [1]

Benefit to plant .... [1]

b. Plant hormones can be used by farmers to manage plant growth.

Give **two** examples of the commercial value of plant hormones.

1. ....

....

2. ....

.... [2]

Language lab

Choose which of the following sentences is the best definition of the term *drug*.

A a chemical substance which affects the nervous system

B a substance which can be obtained from a pharmacy

C a substance taken into the body that affects chemical reactions in the body

D a chemical which is useful as a medicine

1. This table shows the prescription of antibiotics for different medical conditions in a clinic.

medical condition	number of total antibiotic prescriptions
Cholera	8
Tuberculosis	22
Chest infection	110
Food poisoning	56
Gonorrhoea	4

a. Present this information in a suitable fashion. Use the grid below.

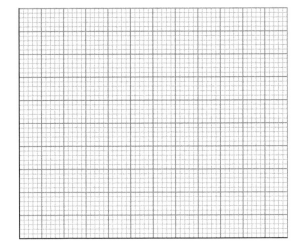

[5]

b. One of the conditions treated is a sexually transmitted infection.

Calculate the percentage of patients treated for this condition.

Show your working.

.... [2]

c. The doctors at the clinic did not want to prescribe antibiotics for influenza.

State **two** reasons why they did not do so.

i. ....

ii. .... [2]

a. Name the organs of gas exchange in mammals.

b. Name the main addictive substance in tobacco smoke.

1. a. Study this histogram.

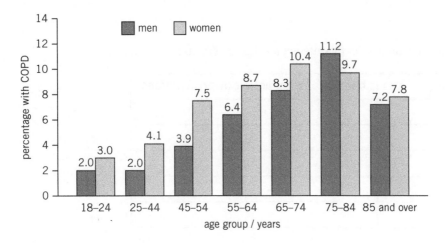

i. Suggest a suitable title for the chart.

.... [1]

ii. State what the initials **COPD** stand for.

.... [1]

iii. Does the chart provide evidence that smoking increases the risk of COPD?

Explain your answer. ....

....

.... [2]

b. The maximum volume of air that can be exchanged with a single breath in and out is called the vital capacity. A typical healthy male would have a vital capacity of about 5000 cm^3.

Describe and explain the likely effect of long-term smoking on vital capacity.

....

....

.... [2]

a. State which mineral ion is required for the production of haemoglobin.

b. Suggest why red blood cells are small and flexible.

1. Cigarette smoke contains carbon monoxide, which can combine with haemoglobin in red blood cells.

   Explain how you would use your biological knowledge and this additional information to persuade a young woman to stop smoking during pregnancy.

   ....

   ....

   .... [2]

2. This bar chart shows a relationship between smoking and lung cancer.

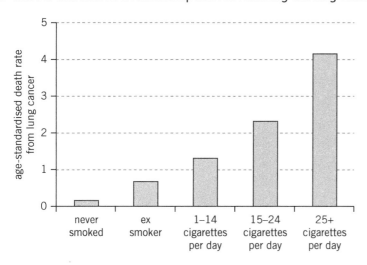

   a. Calculate how much more likely a person who smokes 20 cigarettes per day is to develop lung cancer than a person who has never smoked. Show your working.

   [2]

   b. Some people say that 'just one cigarette a day won't do me any harm'. Use information from the bar chart to help to convince them that this is not the case.

   ....

   ....

   .... [2]

85

Asexual reproduction is the process by which:

A   Four offspring are produced.

B   The offspring are genetically identical.

C   The offspring are genetically different.

D   Only one offspring is produced.

1. The diagrams below show simple schemes for asexual and sexual reproduction.

asexual

sexual

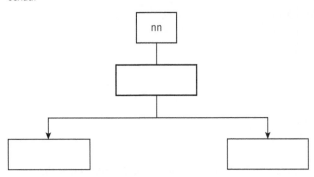

   a. Insert the words **meiosis** and **mitosis** in the correct positions on the diagram.   [2]

   b. Write in the correct chromosome number in the boxes on the diagram.   [2]

   c. Suggest one **advantage** and one **disadvantage** of asexual reproduction in plants.

      Advantage ....

      Disadvantage .... [2]

Language lab

Pollen grains are formed in the:

A carpel

B petal

C anther

D filament

1. **a.** Most of the variations in flower structure are related to the methods of pollination.

Define the term **pollination**. ....

.... [1]

This diagram shows a typical wind-pollinated flower.

   b. Identify the structures labelled **W**, **X**, **Y**, and **Z**.

W...   X ....

Y...   Z .... [4]

2. Complete this table to compare the structure of wind- and insect-pollinated flowers.

part of flower	wind-pollinated	insect-pollinated	explanation
petals			
anthers			
pollen			
stigma			

[8]

A flower is made up of a set of modified leaves. The leaves are arranged in rings which produce the gametes, protect them, and ensure that fertilisation takes place. The rings of leaves are attached to the end of the flower stalk, the receptacle.

Examination of a typical flower

If a typical flower (a buttercup, for example) is examined, it is possible to see the four rings of specialised leaves. It may be necessary to use a hand lens to do this easily.

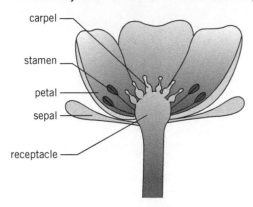

Arrange the four rings (carpel, sepal, stamen, and petal) from outside to inside.

Use a scalpel (take care!) and a pair of forceps to remove a representative part of each ring of leaves. Examine the structure under a hand lens or binocular microscope.

The individual structures will look something like those shown in this diagram.

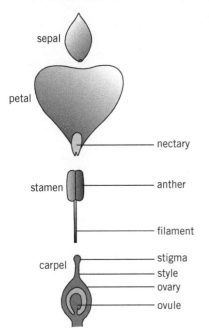

How many of each of the structures can you find in your flower?

Variations in flower structure

Flowers of different species may differ in:

- The number of each of the different components.

- The arrangement of the different parts — especially how fused (stuck together) they are to form tubes or platforms.

Drawing a flower

With so much variation in flower structure, scientists have developed standard ways of describing flower structure. The most common method is to draw a **half flower**.

Use a razor blade or scalpel to cut through the flower, down the line of its stalk. Hold the flower in forceps if necessary, and take care with the sharp blades.

Now draw the flower in section (this gives a three-dimensional view of the petals and sepals).

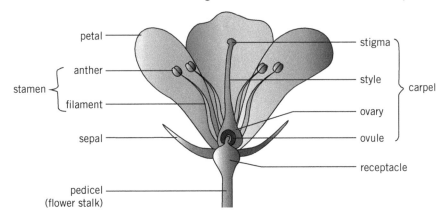

Make sure that the structures are labelled accurately with guide lines drawn with a ruler. (Guide lines always look neater when they are parallel to the top and bottom of the page!)

Add a scale to your drawing.

[6]

Pollination is:

A The transfer of sperm to egg cells.

B The spreading of seeds from a plant.

C The removal of nectar by an insect.

D The transfer of pollen from stamen to stigma of a flower.

1. The diagram below shows half of a tomato flower.

- petal
- anther
- sepal

   a. i. Mark with a **P** the part where a pollen grain must land to pollinate the flower.   [1]

      ii. State the name of the part where the pollen grain has landed.

      .... [1]

   b. This diagram shows a pollen grain with a pollen tube that is growing towards an ovule.

ovule

- pollen grain
- pollen tube
- male nucleus

female nucleus

      i. Complete the drawing of the pollen tube to show how it enters the ovule.   [2]

      ii. Describe and explain what happens to the male and female nucleus at fertilisation.

      ....

      ....

      ....

      .... [3]

Complete this paragraph by filling in the gaps.

A seed contains an .... which can eventually develop into a young plant, a food store which is often

the carbohydrate .... The whole seed is enclosed in a protective coat called the ....

1. The diagram shows a carpel (the female part of a flower).

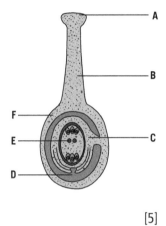

   a. Match the letters on the diagram with the names of structures in this table.

name of structure	label letter
egg cell (female gamete)	
ovule	
style	
stigma	
micropyle	
ovary	

   [5]

   b. Complete the diagram to show how a male nucleus fertilises the egg cell. Add labels to your diagram. [3]

   c. This diagram shows the appearance of a broad bean seed which has been sectioned and stained with iodine solution.

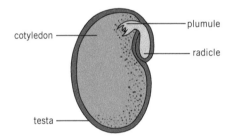

   i. State which parts of the broad bean seed make up the embryo.

   .... [1]

   ii. State the name of the main food material stored in the broad bean seed.

   .... [1]

   iii. Explain what change you would expect to see in the appearance of the seed to make you draw this conclusion.

   .... [1]

If the data collected from an investigation or experiment can be arranged into groups (sometimes called classes) of equal size, then you should draw a histogram.

A **histogram** shows the frequency of data values on a graph. Like a frequency table, data is grouped in intervals of equal size that do not overlap. A histogram differs from a bar graph in that the vertical columns are drawn with no space in between them (see below). Like a bar graph, the height of each bar depicts the frequency of the data values, as long as the bars are the same width.

time spent on the computer / minutes	tally	frequency
0–5	III	3
6–10	III	3
11–15	IMI	5
16–20	IMI III	8
21–25	IMI IMI II	12
26–30	IMI IMI IIII	14
31–35	IMI IMI IMI	15
36–40	IMI IMI I	11
41–45	IIII	4
46–50	IIII	4
51–55	III	3
56–60	II	2

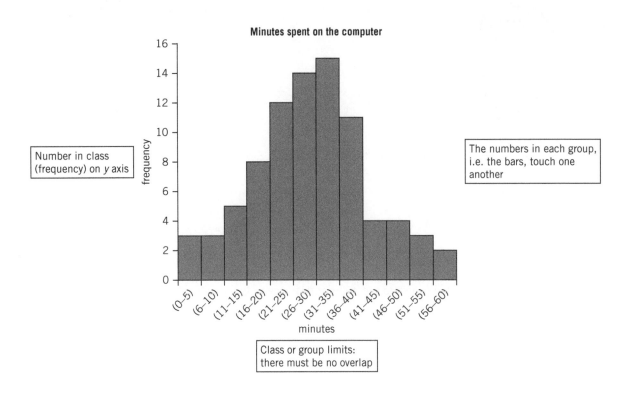

Number in class (frequency) on *y* axis

The numbers in each group, i.e. the bars, touch one another

Class or group limits: there must be no overlap

Suggest two features of humans which show continuous variation, so could be plotted on a histogram like the one below.

1. A broad bean fruit (a pod) contains several seeds. A student opened up 50 broad bean pods and counted the number of seeds in each. He recorded his results in a tally chart.

number of seeds in pod	4	5	6	7	8
tally	II	Ⅲ Ⅲ	Ⅲ Ⅲ Ⅲ Ⅲ II	Ⅲ Ⅲ Ⅲ	I
total number					

a. Complete the table to show the number of pods containing each number of seeds. [1]

b. Present these results in a suitable graph. Use the grid provided below.

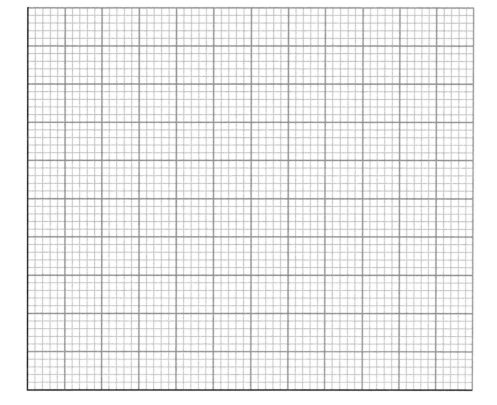

[4]

c. State the most frequent number of seeds in a pod. .... [1]

d. Calculate the percentage of pods which contain the most common number of seeds. Show your working.

.....................................% [2]

Language lab

Which statement is true for both eggs and sperm?

A They are both motile.

B They are produced throughout life.

C They both produce hormones.

D They contain the haploid number of chromosomes.

1. This diagram shows the reproductive system of a human male.

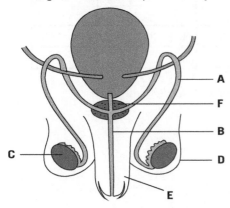

a. State the names of the parts labelled **A, B, C, D, E,** and **F**.

Write your answers in the table below.

A	
B	
C	
D	
E	
F	

[6]

b. Use the letters to state:

i. the part which produces the male gametes .... [1]

ii. the part which produces the liquid part of semen .... [1]

iii. the part which produces testosterone .... [1]

iv. the part which also carries urine .... [1]

v. the part which is cut during the process of vasectomy. .... [1]

c. Arrange the following processes into the correct sequence necessary for the production of a human baby.

A ejaculation   **B** implantation   **C** birth

D fertilisation   **E** ovulation   **F** development

....   [3]

The site of gamete formation in the human female is the:

A uterus

B ovary

C oviduct

D vagina

1. This diagram shows the human female reproductive system.

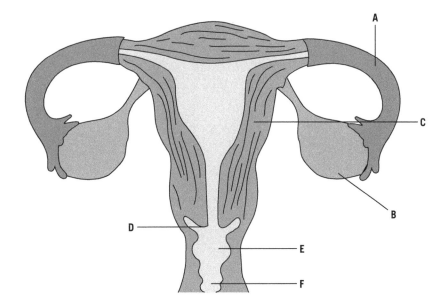

Use the letters to state:

a. the part which produces the female gametes   .... [1]

b. the part where fertilisation normally occurs   .... [1]

c. the part where sperm are deposited during intercourse   .... [1]

d. the part where implantation occurs   .... [1]

e. the part where a contraceptive diaphragm is placed.   .... [1]

Language lab

Fertility may be controlled by IVF and by AI. What do these abbreviations mean?

[1]

1. The diagram below shows the changes in concentration of four hormones during the menstrual cycle.

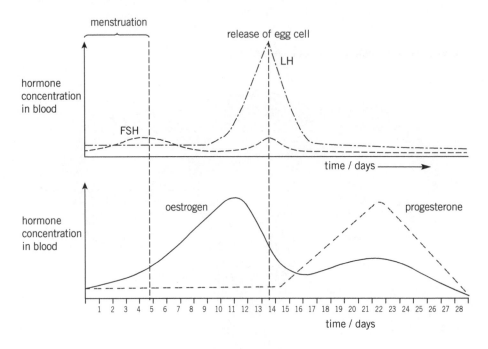

a. Oestrogen is known to inhibit the production of FSH by feedback inhibition of the action of the pituitary gland, and FSH is known to stimulate development of mature eggs in the ovary. Progesterone inhibits formation of both LH and FSH.

Use the graph, and the information above, to explain how one or more of these hormones might be used to treat infertility.

....

....

....

.... [3]

b. Suggest which hormone might be useful in preparation for IVF. Explain your answer.

.... because ....

.... [2]

c. Women who are lactating produce high levels of oestrogen. Suggest how this might act as a natural method of contraception.

....

.... [1]

The period of time between conception and birth is called:

A   gestation period   B   menstrual cycle

C   parturition phase   D   ovulation

1. The diagram below shows a human uterus containing a developing fetus.

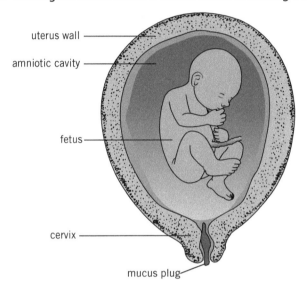

a. i. Name two structures shown in the diagram which protect the fetus.

   For each structure you have named, explain how it carries out its protective function.

   Structure 1: name .... [1]

   Explanation of function ....

   .... [1]

   Structure 2: name .... [1]

   Explanation of function ....

   .... [1]

   ii. Draw in the position of the placenta on this diagram.   [1]

b. Complete this table by placing a tick (✓) in ONE box on each line to show the movement, if any, of each substance across the placenta.

substance	from mother to fetus	from fetus to mother	no movement across placenta
glucose			
haemoglobin			
nicotine			
amino acids			
carbon dioxide			
alcohol			
urea			

[7]

Complete the following paragraph.

The phase of human development in which an individual becomes capable of producing mature sex cells is called

.... This process is closely controlled by ....

which bring about physical changes called the .... characteristics.

1. The diagram shows some of the changes associated with puberty.

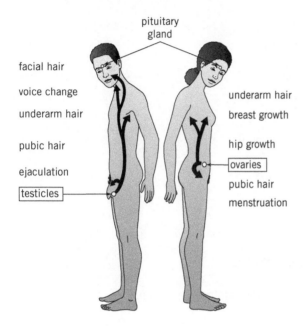

     a. i. Name the gland which first provides the signals to begin the changes associated with puberty.

.... [1]

     ii. Name the hormone responsible for these changes in a male.

.... [1]

     b. Suggest why the breasts grow bigger and the hips grow wider as a female passes puberty.

Breasts ....

Hips .... [2]

     c. Menstruation is a sign of the monthly menstrual cycles.

State the name of the end of active menstrual cycles in the female.

.... [1]

HIV is an organism which can be transmitted by sexual activity. This organism is harmful because it affects which type of cell?

A egg cells

B red blood cells

C white blood cells

D brain cells

1. Gonorrhoea is a sexually transmitted infection (an STI).

   a. i. State which **type** of organism causes gonorrhoea.

   .... [1]

   ii. State **one** early symptom of gonorrhoea.

   .... [1]

   iii. State which method of contraception is most likely to prevent transmission of this disease.

   .... [1]

   b. Another STI is AIDS.

   i. Explain how AIDS affects the human body.

   .... [2]

   ii. Explain why AIDS and gonorrhoea cannot be treated by the same drugs.

   .... [2]

A section of DNA which codes for a single protein is a:

A chromosome   **B** nucleus

C gamete   **D** gene

1. The diagram shows a short sequence of bases in a DNA molecule. The base sequence in DNA carries information in the form of a genetic code.

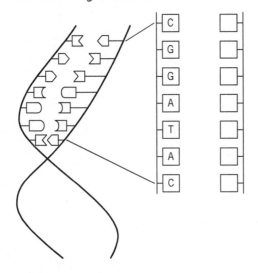

a. Write down the sequence of bases on the other strand of the DNA molecule.   [2]

b. A modified copy of the DNA sequence is carried to the cytoplasm of the cell.

  i. State the name of this modified sequence. .... [1]

  ii. State the name of the structure in the cell where the code is 'read' by the cell. .... [1]

c. A sequence of three bases carries a code for another type of biological molecule.

  State the name of this type of molecule. .... [1]

d. The type of molecule named in your answer to part **c** is built up into larger molecules, and these molecules determine the characteristics of organisms.

  i. State the general name given to these larger molecules. .... [1]

  ii. Complete this table to match the molecules to their functions (i.e. to the characteristics they give to an organism).   [5]

molecule	characteristic
	ability of red blood cells to transport oxygen
	bind to and identify molecules on the surface of invading microbes
receptor protein in synapse	
lipase	
	provides strength and structure to hair and nails

Language lab

State what the initials DNA stand for.

Suggest two pieces of information we can gain from this name.

1. Here is a list of statements about DNA. State whether each of the statements is true or false.

statement	true	false
DNA carries coded instructions for the characteristics of an organism		
DNA is only found in the nucleus of cells of vertebrate animals		
DNA is a large molecule, but its code is carried in only four different subunits		
A DNA profile can be used to identify a criminal		
DNA can be extracted from dead dinosaurs		
Plant cells have different DNA to animal cells		
One difference between animals and bacteria is that bacteria do not have DNA		
The DNA profile is unique to each individual human		
50 human cheek cells fit into a 1 mm space, but each cheek cell contains 2 m of DNA		
Zoo scientists can copy the DNA found in an orang-utan, and check if it is related to an orang-utan at another zoo		

2. Genetic engineers can produce Golden Rice.

   State which **one** of the following is a benefit of this process. [1]

   A   the golden colour of the rice attracts pollinating insects

   B   the rice contains high levels of ß-carotene, which can be converted to vitamin D

   C   the rice contains high levels of ß-carotene, which can be converted to vitamin A

   D   the engineered rice is resistant to herbicide sprays

3. The genetic material of a coronavirus like SARS-cov-2 is RNA not DNA.

   State two differences between the structures of RNA and DNA.

   ....

   .... [2]

Language lab

DNA carries the code for protein synthesis.

State which of the following is the correct sequence of events in this process.

A   mRNA → transcription → translation → chain of amino acids → DNA

B   DNA → translation → mRNA → transcription → amino acid chain

C   DNA → transcription → mRNA → translation → amino acid chain

D   amino acid chain → translation → mRNA → transcription → DNA   [1]

1. Chromosomes contain DNA. Each individual, with very few exceptions, has different DNA. The DNA can be broken up, and the pieces used to produce a 'genetic fingerprint'. The diagram shows the genetic fingerprints of blood found at a murder scene and from blood samples provided by five suspects.

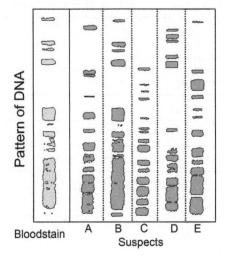

Fill in the missing words in the following sentences.

a.   the chromosomes are found in the .... of the cell.   [1]

b.   genetic fingerprints must be made from the .... blood cells of the suspect   [1]

c.   the murderer was most likely to be suspect ....   [1]

d.   genetic fingerprints can only be identical if they come from ....   [1]

e.   Genetic fingerprinting can also be useful in other ways. Suggest how DNA fingerprinting could be valuable in

   i.   prevention of dangerous inbreeding in rare animals kept in zoos.

   ....

   ....   [2]

   ii.   classification of living organisms collected from a new environment.

   ....

   ....   [2]

   f.   There are four different bases in DNA. A codon is made of three bases.

      State how many different codons can be produced. ....   [1]

When a human cell with 46 chromosomes divides by mitosis it will produce:

A   one cell with 46 chromosomes

B   two cells with 23 chromosomes each

C   two cells with 46 chromosomes each

D   four cells with 23 chromosomes each

1. Human body cells usually contain 23 pairs of chromosomes. The exceptions to this rule are the gametes and the mature red blood cells.

   a. Complete the table below.

type of cell	total number of chromosomes	type of sex chromosomes present
male nerve cell		
female white blood cell		
sperm cell		
egg cell/ovum		
red blood cell		

[5]

   b. Blood cells are produced in bone marrow. State the name of the type of cell division which produces them.

   .... [1]

2. This diagram shows some stages in cell division.

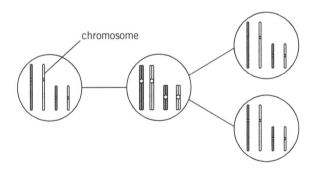

chromosome

   a. State the diploid number of chromosomes in these cells. .... [1]

   b. Name the type of cell division shown. .... [1]

   c. Give **two** examples of sites where this type of cell division occurs.

   1. ....

   2. .... [2]

Which **two** of the following cells do not contain a diploid nucleus?

A   an egg cell and a muscle cell

B   a red blood cell and a sperm cell

C   a sperm cell and a nerve cell

D   a muscle cell and a red blood cell

1. The photomicrograph shows a set of chromosomes during meiosis.

   a. Complete the diagram below by drawing in the chromosomes of the four cells produced when the original cell divides by meiosis.

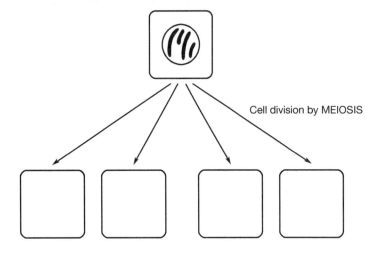

Cell division by MEIOSIS

[4]

   b. State the site of meiosis in:

     i. a mammal .... [1]

     ii. a flowering plant. .... [1]

   c. Explain why it is necessary for gametes to be produced by meiosis.

....

....

[2]

In humans the allele for brown eyes (B) is dominant to the allele for blue eyes (b). If one parent is represented as BB and the other as Bb, then they will both:

A have brown eyes but different genotypes

B have blue eyes and the same genotypes

C have the same phenotypes and genotypes

D be heterozygous with brown eyes

1. This paragraph describes some features of inheritance.

   Use words from this list to complete each of the spaces in the paragraph. Each word may be used once, or not at all.

   allele   diploid   discontinuous   dominant   gene   haploid   heterozygous
   homozygous   meiosis   mitosis   recessive   redundant

   In humans, eye colour may be brown or blue. This is controlled by a single .... which has two forms.

   Gametes are formed by the type of cell division called .... : the gametes are

   .... and fuse at .... to form a

   .... zygote.

   Two humans both have brown eyes, but one of their three children has blue eyes. This means that blue eye colour is

   controlled by a .... allele and that both of the parents are .... [7]

2. Study the two lists below. One is a list of genetic terms and the other is a list of definitions of these terms.

   Draw guidelines to link each term with its correct definition.

genetic term	definition
genotype	the observable features of an organism
homozygous	an allele that is always expressed if it is present
dominant	having two alternative alleles of a gene
heterozygous	one alternative form of a gene
recessive	the set of alleles present in an organism
chromosome	having two identical alleles
allele	a thread-like structure of DNA, carrying genetic information in the form of genes
phenotype	two identical alleles of a particular gene

[8]

A couple who are both carriers (heterozygous) for a fatal genetic condition might be advised not to have children because:

A   all of their children will show the condition

B   the child's genes are more likely to mutate

C   the child could receive the recessive allele from each parent

D   the mother could be harmed during the pregnancy

1. Tongue rolling is an example of discontinuous variation. It is partly controlled by a dominant allele, R, of a single gene.

   a. i. Name one other example of discontinuous variation in humans.

   .... [1]

   ii. Define the term *allele*.

   .... [1]

   iii. Draw a simple labelled diagram to show how genes and chromosomes are related to one another.   [2]

   b. This diagram shows a family history (a pedigree) of tongue rolling over three generations.

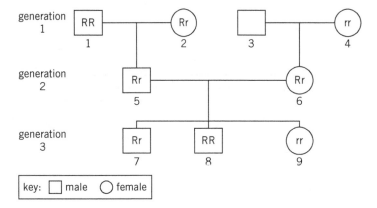

   i. State which individual in generation 3 is *not* a tongue roller. .... [1]

   ii. Suggest the possible phenotypes of individual 3. .... [1]

   iii. Individual 7 marries a woman who is heterozygous for tongue rolling.

      State the probability (chance) that their second child will be a tongue roller.

   .... [1]

In one family, there were four children with different blood groups, i.e. A, B, AB, and O. Which one of the following combinations were the parent's genotypes?

A   AO and BO

B   AB and OO

C   AB and AB

D   AO and AB

1. a. A set of triplets was born, but their mother died during the birth. The babies were separated from one another, and brought up by different families. When they were 18 they met up with one another for the first time since their separation. Various measurements were made on them, and some of the information obtained is recorded in this table.

	Andrew	John	David
mass / kg	81	92	86
height / cm	179	180	179
blood group	O	O	AB
intelligence quotient (IQ)	128	138	140

i. State which two of the boys might be identical twins from this evidence.

.... and .... [1]

ii. Explain which piece of evidence is most important in helping you to reach this conclusion.

....

.... [1]

iii. Suggest a reason why Andrew and David have such different body mass measurements although they are of the same height.

.... [1]

b. The ABO blood group is determined by three alleles, although only two are present in any one cell. The three alleles are given the symbols I^A, I^B, and I^O.

The relationship between genotype and phenotype for these blood groups is shown in the table below.

genotype	$I^A I^A$	$I^A I^O$	$I^B I^B$	$I^B I^O$	$I^A I^B$	$I^O I^O$
phenotype	A	A	B	B	AB	O

State the name of this type of genetic relationship, in which a particular combination of alleles (in this case $I^A I^B$) results in a new phenotype.

.... [1]

N is the allele for normal colour vision, and **n** is the allele for red-green colour blindness. An individual with the genotype $X^N X^n$ is:

A   a boy with normal colour vision   **B**   a colour blind boy

C   a colour blind girl   **D**   a girl who is a carrier for colour blindness

1. Haemophilia is a sex-linked inherited disease. It is controlled by alleles carried on the X chromosome (**H** for normal clotting, **h** for haemophilia).

The table below gives some information about possible combinations of phenotype and genotype.

Complete the table by:

a. drawing the correct chromosomes in boxes 2, 3, and 5

b. adding the symbols for the alleles to the correct positions on the chromosomes

c. writing into the final row the sex of each individual.

	possible combinations				
	1	2	3	4	5
diagram	H—⧗⧗—H			H—⧗ ⧗	
sex chromosomes	XX	XX	XX	XY	XY
sex of person					

[5]

d. The genotype of individuals showing the normal clotting condition can be represented as:

Normal male $X^H Y$ Normal female $X^H X^H$

i. State the genotype of a carrier female .... [1]

ii. Complete the Punnett Square below to show the results of a cross between a carrier female and a normal male

Gametes Female Male		

[4]

iii. What is the probability that a child from such a cross would be a male haemophiliac?

.... [1]

Complete the following paragraph.

The sum of the characteristics of an organism is called its ...., and results from a combination of its set of genes (its ....) and the effects of the ....

1. Study the two lists below. One is a list of terms relating to variation and the other is a list of definitions of these terms.

    Draw guidelines to link each term with its correct definition.

genetic term		definition
continuous variation		the observable features of an organism
gene		a form of variation with many intermediate forms between the extremes
discontinuous variation		one possible form of environmental influence on variation
phenotype		one example of discontinuous variation
height in humans		this factor, in addition to genotype, can affect phenotype
environment		a section of DNA responsible for an inherited characteristic
nutrients		one example of continuous variation
blood group		a form of variation with clear-cut differences between groups

[8]

2. Charles Darwin believed that new **species** can arise by natural selection of variations within a population. Since Darwin's time, scientists have suggested that variation may arise by **mutation**, as well as by the formation of new combinations of **genes** at fertilisation during sexual reproduction.

    a. State the meanings of the terms

        i.   species .... [1]

        ii. mutation .... [1]

        iii. gene .... [1]

    b. Suggest **two** factors which may increase the rate of mutation in a population

        1. ....

        2. .... [2]

State one important difference between discontinuous and continuous variation.

1. Jack and Salim were working together on a mathematical investigation. They decided to measure the body masses of each of the other students in their class.

   The results are shown in this table.

mass category / kg	tally of number in group	number in group
35–38	I	
39–42	II	
43–46	IIII	
47–50	₦ I	
51–54	₦ ₦	
55–58	₦	
59–62	III	
63–66	II	
67–70	I	

   a. Complete the third column of the table by adding up the tally numbers.   [2]

   b. Plot these results in a suitable form on the grid below.

   [5]

   c. State which form of variation this graph illustrates. .... [1]

   d. Explain how this form of variation comes about. ....

   .... [2]

Complete the following sentence.

.... is a change in structure of an organism to suit it to its environment, and results from

an alteration in an organism's .... (its set of genes).

1. a. The table below shows some examples of selection.

example	type of selection: natural or artificial
Cattle being bred that are able to withstand cold winters.	
The development of a strain of rice that is more resistant to disease.	
The resistance of a strain of bacteria to a particular antibiotic.	
The ability of a species of shrub to grow on soil containing high amounts of copper.	
The similarity between a moth's wing pattern and its habitat, making it less conspicuous to predatory birds.	

Complete the table to show which type of selection, natural, or artificial, is involved.   [5]

b. The bar graph shows the average milk yield for a herd of Friesian cows between 1976 and 2004.

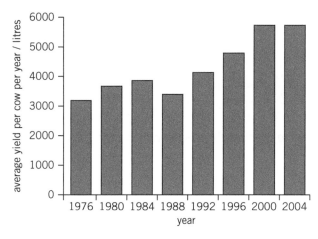

i. Explain how animal breeders might have caused the trend between 1976 and 2004 to occur.

....

....

.... [3]

ii. Apart from the yield of food (milk or meat), suggest another characteristic that farmers might improve in animals to make a farm more economically successful.

.... [1]

111

The dark form of the peppered moth lives mainly in industrial areas because it:

A is a mutant

B is well camouflaged from its natural predators

C can only find suitable breeding sites in such areas

D can find food more easily in industrial areas

1. The Everglades is an enormous flooded area in southern Florida, USA.

    There are many different species of animals and plants there, and they are well adapted to their environment.

    a. The animals and plants have become well adapted by the process of natural selection.

        The following are stages in the evolution of species by means of natural selection.

        A survival of the best adapted

        B over-production of offspring

        C competition causes a struggle for existence

        D advantageous characteristics are passed on to offspring

        E variation occurs between members of the same population

        Use the letters **A–E** to rearrange these stages into the correct sequence.

        …..   …..   …..   …..   …..   [5]

    b. Some of the early European explorers in Florida noticed that there were many species of bird.

        The heads and beaks of birds are often well adapted to their diet. The diagrams in this table show the heads of some species of birds.

        Draw guidelines to match up the heads with the likely diet of the birds.

| Feeds on nuts and other hard fruits | Filters algae and other small organisms from the water | Feeds by spearing fish and frogs | Captures Florida rabbits and other mammals | Feeds by catching small insects |

[5]

Complete the following paragraph.

All spaniels belong to the same .... but may be very different in appearance as a result of

....

1. a. The diagrams below show the effect of selective breeding on wild cabbage (*Brassica oleracea*).

flower

garden cabbage

bud

leaf

brussels sprouts

wild cabbage

broccoli

State which part of the wild cabbage has been selected for when breeding the:

brussels sprouts ....

broccoli .... [2]

   b. Once a plant has been selected as a new variety of broccoli, the grower then produces many more identical plants by taking cuttings.

   i. Explain why the cuttings grow to be identical to the parent plant.

   ....

   ....

   .... [2]

   ii. The cuttings are usually planted into a type of compost containing plant hormones (to encourage rooting) and additional nitrate. The cuttings are kept in a closed transparent enclosure.

   Explain the importance of:

   nitrate in the growth compost ....

   .... [1]

   keeping the plants in a closed environment. ....

   .... [1]

The energy flowing through an ecosystem arrives from:

A combustion of fuels

B solar energy from the Sun

C nuclear power stations

D geothermal energy from volcanoes

1. a. This diagram represents the energy flow through a food chain.

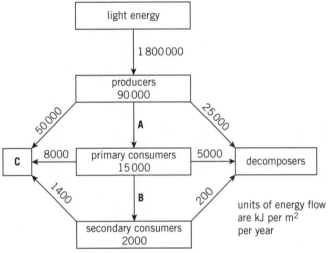

i. Name the source of light energy. .... [1]

ii. State the process occurring at **A** and **B**. .... [1]

iii. Explain why not all of the light energy available is absorbed by the producers.

....

.... [2]

iv. State the name of the process shown at **C**, and the form in which the energy is lost.

Process .... [1]

Form of energy lost .... [1]

b. i. Calculate the percentage of energy transferred at stages **A** and **B**.

Show your working.

A .... **B** .... [2]

ii. Suggest how evidence in the diagram supports the idea that humans should eat more vegetable matter and less meat.

....

....

....

.... [3]

Complete the following sentence.

In producing a pyramid of biomass, the biomass is calculated by multiplying .... and ....

1. Feeding relationships.

   Use guide lines to match the terms with their definitions.

term/process
food chain

definition
an organism that gets its energy from dead or waste organic material

term/process
food web

definition
an organism that gets its energy by feeding on other organisms

term/process
producer

definition
an animal that gets its energy by eating other animals

term/process
consumer

definition
a network of interconnected food chains

term/process
herbivore

definition
the transfer of energy from one organism to the next, beginning with a producer

term/process
carnivore

definition
an organism that makes its own organic nutrients, usually through photosynthesis

term/process
decomposer

definition
an animal that gets its energy from eating plants

2. A group of students studied a food web for an English lake.

   Algae are small microscopic plants. Water fleas are small crustaceans about 2 mm in length. Smelt are fish – they are adult at about 4 cm in length. The kingfisher is a bird, about 22 cm long.

   Draw and label a likely pyramid of numbers for the food chain linking:

   algae ⟶ water fleas ⟶ smelt ⟶ kingfisher

[2]

Language lab

The energy content of a piece of biological material can be measured in:

A kilojoules   B kilograms

C degrees   D watts

1. The image shows sheep feeding on dried pellet food.

The pellets of food are made by collecting seeds and grains from crop plants, and drying them.

Humans eat some of the sheep.

a. Explain why it would be more efficient if humans ate the grains and seeds instead of meat from the sheep.

....

....

....

.... [3]

b. The sheep are often kept inside heated sheds. Explain why this might save money for the farmer.

....

....

....

.... [3]

Fill in the gaps.

The simplest carbon cycle would involve an approximate balance between two processes,

.... and ....

1. The first part of this question asks you to use a list of words to fill in a set of boxes. This is quite a common way to test your knowledge and understanding of a biological process. The diagram below represents the carbon cycle.

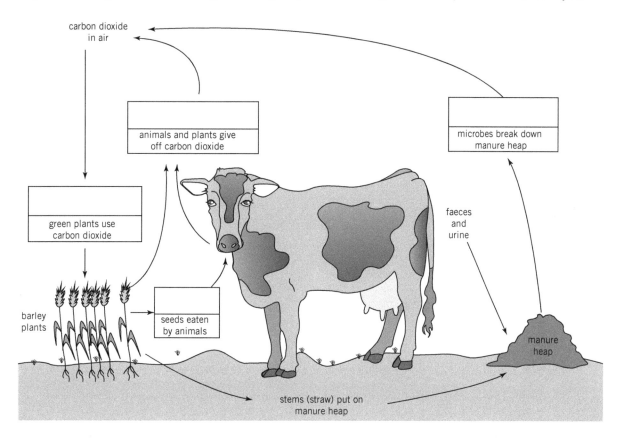

a. Use words from this list to complete the boxes in the diagram.

   combustion   decay   excretion   feeding   photosynthesis   respiration [4]

b. In some countries the manure heap is collected, dried, and then burned as a fuel.

   State the effect that this would have on the carbon dioxide concentration in the air.

   .... [1]

Language lab

Complete the following sentence.

During the process of denitirification, ... is changed

to .... by ....

1. a. The diagram shows the nitrogen cycle.

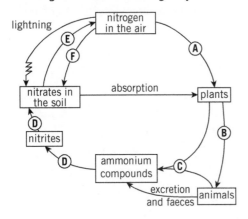

i. Name the processes **B** and **E**.

B ....

E .... [2]

ii. Name the process and the organisms involved in **C**.

Process ....

Organisms .... [2]

b. A heap of dead leaves had been left to decompose. Part of the decomposition sequence is shown below.

Use this sequence and your own knowledge to answer the following questions.

i. Suggest **three** effects on the sequence if the *Nitrosomonas* bacteria died out.

1. ....

2. ....

3. .... [3]

ii. Tick **two** boxes in this table to show factors which would speed up the decomposition process.

factor	box
maintaining an acid pH	
a plastic cover to exclude air	
few scavenging insects	
many scavenging insects	
regular turning of the heap to add air	

[2]

118

Arrange the following phases of a population curve into the correct sequence:
lag – decline – stationary – exponential

1. This diagram shows a number of factors that can affect the size of a population.

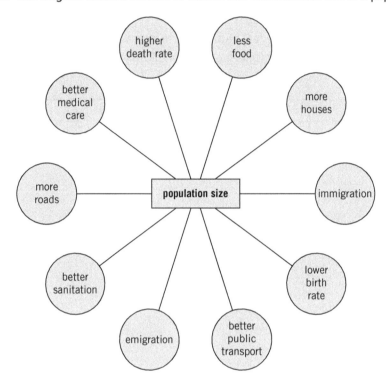

a. State **four** factors, shown in the diagram, that reduce the size of a population.

....

....

....

.... [4]

b. Suggest **two** ways in which better medical care can lead to an increase in the size of a population.

....

.... [2]

c. State **two** ways in which humans control bacterial populations. [1]

....

.... [2]

Language lab

> Fill in the gaps.
>
> Bacteria are examples of .... because they do not have a
>
> .... They do have a .... but it
>
> is not made of cellulose. They can reproduce very quickly as each cell can split into two – this process is called
>
> ....

1. An experiment was carried out to follow the population growth of the bacterium *Escherichia coli*.

   Cells of the bacterium were placed in a flask containing sterile nutrient broth and then incubated at 30°C. Every five hours a sample was removed from the flask, and the number of bacteria present was calculated.

   The results are shown in this table.

time from start / h	5	10	15	20	25	30	35	40	45	50
number of bacteria / millions per cm³	20	50	430	450	460	420	220	55	20	0

   a. Draw a graph of these results on the grid below.

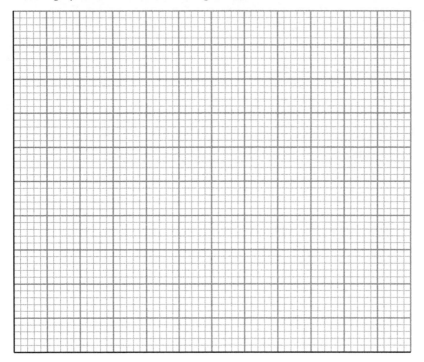

   b. Suggest why the nutrient broth:

      contains sugar .... [1]

      contains amino acids .... [1]

      must be sterile. ....

      .... [2]

   c. Mark with a letter **R** on the graph the period during the experiment when the rate of reproduction was at its greatest. [1]

   d. Suggest **two** possible reasons why the population declined between 25 and 50 hours. [1]

      ....

      .... [2]

Which one of the following is not a major source of dietary carbohydrate?

A potatoes   B rice

C wheat   D milk

1. a. This set of pie charts shows the food groups present in eggs, milk, rice, and beans.

   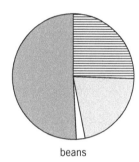

eggs   milk   rice   beans

key to food groups

▤ water   ☐ proteins   ☐ fats and oils   ▨ carbohydrates

A malnourished person may have an unbalanced diet that may be missing some essential nutrients.

i. State which food has the highest concentration of protein. .... [1]

ii. State which food has the most carbohydrate. .... [1]

iii. Name **two** other food groups not shown in the pie charts.

....

.... [2]

b. An extreme and continued shortage of food can result in a famine.

State **three** factors which may cause this shortage of food.

1. ....

2. ....

3. .... [3]

Fill in the gaps.

Deforestation reduces the availability of .... for many birds and increases the

risk of .... erosion.

1. More food and raw materials are required to meet the demands of an increasing world population.

   Describe and explain the possible harmful effects on organisms and the environment of burning large areas of Indonesian rainforest, so that the land can be used to grow palm oil trees.

   ....

   ....

   .... [4]

2. These diagrams show changes to a farm between 1953 and 2003.

   key
   hedges —— boundary - - - -
   river ⌒⌒ buildings ■ ■
   trees ✤ ✤ marsh ⚵ ⚵ ⚵

   The fields on the farm are separated by hedges.

   a. i. State **two** major changes which were made to the land between 1953 and 2003.

       1. ....

       ....

       2. ....

       .... [2]

   ii. Suggest and explain **two** ways in which these changes would affect wildlife on the farm.

       1. ....

       ....

       2. ....

       .... [4]

   b. Farmers often remove areas of woodland to provide more space for growing crops.

       Suggest **three** disadvantages of this deforestation.

       1. ....

       2. ....

       3. .... [3]

Two pollutants produced by car engines are:

A sulfur dioxide and nitrogen oxides   **B** oil and water

C methane and carbon dioxide   **D** sulfur dioxide and methane

1. The table below provides some data about a number of atmospheric gases.

name of gas	source(s) of gas	percentage influence on greenhouse effect
CFCs	air conditioning systems; aerosol propellant; refrigerators	13
carbon dioxide	burning forest trees; burning fossil fuels; production of cement	56
nitrous oxide	breakdown of fertilisers	6
methane	waste gases from animals such as sheep, cattle, and termites; rotting vegetation	25

a. Explain why these gases are called 'greenhouse' gases.

....

....

.... [2]

b. From this data suggest why the following practices should be encouraged:

1. Development of renewable energy resources such as wind turbines

.... [1]

2. Improved insulation of walls and roofs in houses

.... [1]

3. Reforestation

.... [1]

2. There are large copper mines in Tanzania. One of these mines is so far from railway links that all supplies must be brought in, and all products and waste materials removed, by trucks. These trucks run throughout the day and night.

Describe and explain the possible harmful effects on organisms and the environment.

....

....

.... [3]

Language lab

> Inorganic fertilisers can be harmful to living organisms because they:
>
> **A** are washed into rivers and pollute the water
>
> **B** remain in the soil and poison soil animals
>
> **C** decompose and pollute the air
>
> **D** can be absorbed through the skin of animals

1. Organisms in a lake or river can be affected by pollution. The statements below describe some of the effects on organisms of sewage being allowed to run into the water.

   The statements are in the wrong order.

statement	letter
Plants on the bottom of the lake die	A
Algae near the surface of the lake absorb nitrates and grow in large numbers	B
Sewage flows into the lake from a nearby farm	C
Increased algae prevent light from reaching plants rooted at the bottom of the lake	D
Bacteria break down the sewage into nitrates	E

   a. Rearrange the letters to show the correct sequence of events. The first one has been done for you.

sequence of events	first step	second step	third step	fourth step	fifth step
letter	C				

   [4]

   b. Suggest one other source of nitrates which may enter the lake.

   .... [1]

   c. The sequence that you have described in your answer to part **a** is not the end of the harmful events that may take place.

   Describe three further steps to show how aerobic bacteria may cause the death of fish and larger invertebrates in the lake.

   1. ....

   2. ....

   3. .... [3]

The two most significant greenhouse gases are .... and

....

1. Biotechnology has made it possible to use algae as a source of fuel.

   The algae are grown in a vessel called a biocoil, then dried and ground up to form a powder, which can be used as fuel.

   The biocoil is a transparent tube about 5 m high, and the algae constantly circulate through it in a nutrient solution. The algae grow and multiply at a very fast rate.

   The diagram shows the main stages in this process.

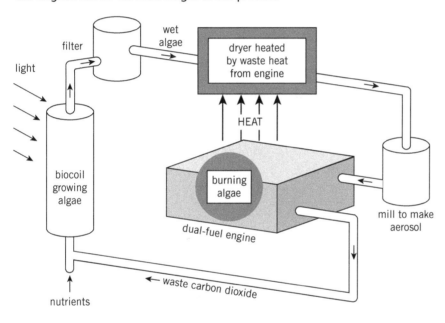

   a. Write out an equation to summarise how energy is trapped by the algae.   [2]

   b. Explain why it is essential that the biocoil is transparent.

      ....

      ....

      .... [2]

   c. Explain why it is essential to use an organism with a high rate of reproduction in this process.

      ....

      ....

      .... [2]

Language lab

In an area where starchy food is plentiful but there is little meat or fish, farmers might be advised to grow:

A cereals

B potatoes

C legumes

D citrus fruits

1. a. Modern fishing boats use ultrasound equipment to locate shoals of fish, and giant nets with very small mesh to capture their prey.

Describe and explain the possible harmful effects on organisms and the environment.

....

....

....

.... [3]

b. Until recent times, fishing in the North Sea was largely unrestricted.

Suggest **three** measures that could be taken to help to conserve the cod population.

1. ....

....

2. ....

....

3. ....

.... [3]

2. a. Fish are a good source of protein. Describe a simple chemical test for this molecule.

....

.... [2]

b. Fish liver is a good source of vitamin D. Explain why this is an important part of the human diet.

....

.... [2]

Language lab

Fill in the gaps.

A species may become endangered by loss of ...., by hunting,

and by failure to .... quickly enough (to replace individuals that die).

1. Define the term *conservation*. ....

.... [2]

2. **a.** The giant panda (*Ailuropoda melanoleuca*) is an endangered species.

   i. Suggest and explain **two** reasons why the panda is endangered. One reason should relate to the environment, and one reason should relate to the biology of the panda itself.

   Environmental factor .... Explanation of effect ....

   .... [2]

   Biological factor .... Explanation of effect ....

   .... [2]

   ii. The giant panda is sometimes called a **flagship species**. Explain what is meant by a flagship species.

   ....

   .... [2]

   b. A conservation management plan involves several steps. The first step is to sample the population of the endangered species.

   i. Explain why sampling is necessary. ....

   .... [2]

   ii. For any named species, suggest a suitable method of sampling.

   Name of species ....

   Method of sampling ....

   .... [2]

127

Fill in the gaps.

Conservation maintains .... (the number of different species in a habitat).

It will involve careful management by ....

1. A farmer believes in sustainable farming.

   a. What is meant by the term **sustainable**? ....

   .... [1]

   The farmer plants a forest of young fir trees. Ten years later the forest is thinned by removing some of the trees. A small part of the forest is harvested in each of the following years.

   b. Suggest **two** advantages of thinning the forest.

   ....

   .... [2]

   c. Suggest **two** disadvantages of growing trees as a monoculture.

   ....

   .... [2]

   d. This list contains some properties of trees. A farmer buying young trees would consider these properties when making his purchase.

fast growth	**good growth on poor soil**	**high quality of wood pulp**
	low cost	**resistance to disease**

   Choose any **three** of these properties and suggest a reason why each property would be useful to the farmer.

property	reason for choice

Language lab

Fill the gaps.

Most soft drink cans contain the metal .... The supply of metals like this one is limited,

so the metal should be ....

[2]

1. a. The diagram shows some of the stages in paper manufacture and recycling.

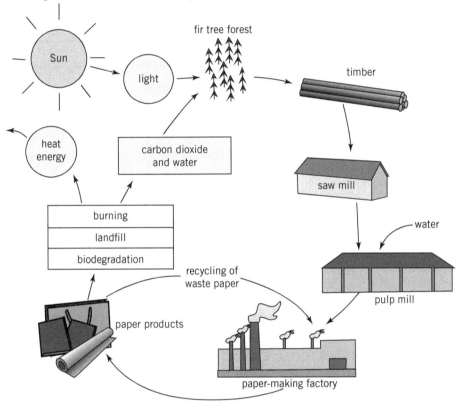

i. Name the process used by the trees to manufacture sugars.

.... [1]

ii. Name the process by which carbon dioxide leaves the trees.

.... [1]

iii. In the mill the wood pulp is treated with sodium hydroxide to break down the fibres in the wood.

State the effect on the pH of the pulp. .... [1]

b. i. One of the paper products manufactured in the paper-making factory is paper bags. Give **two** reasons why paper bags are more environmentally friendly than plastic bags.

....

.... [2]

ii. Suggest **two** other uses of recycled waste paper.

....

.... [2]

A small piece of DNA that can be moved from one bacterial cell to another is a:

A gene   **B** enzyme

C ribosome   **D** plasmid

1. **a.** For each of the following statements, mark as True (T) or False (F).

	statement	True or False
1	A typical bacterium is about one thousandth of a metre wide	
2	Bacteria are smaller than viruses	
3	Gonorrhoea is caused by a bacterium	
4	Bacteria may contain plasmids	
5	All bacteria are harmful	
6	Bacteria multiply by binary fission	
7	A bacterium called *Vibrio* causes cholera	
8	Bacteria can produce the enzyme protease	
9	Bacteria can be genetically modified to produce human insulin	
10	Some bacteria can produce their own organic chemicals using energy from the Sun	
11	Bacteria in the human intestine produce some of the vitamins required for human health	
12	Bacteria have a nucleus, but it is smaller than a human nucleus	

[12]

b. For any three of the statements which you have labelled as False, explain why you have made that choice.

1. Statement ....

Explanation ....

.... [2]

2. Statement ....

Explanation ....

.... [2]

3. Statement ....

Explanation ....

.... [2]

An important enzyme involved in clearing fruit juices is ....

1. The diagram shows a piece of equipment used in one commercial use of enzymes.

Some enzymes are **immobilised** on a carrier of fibres. They can be re-used many times eg. lactase for lactose-free milk

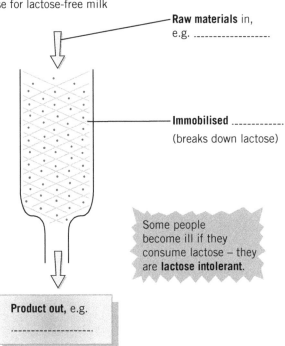

Raw materials in, e.g. -------------------

Immobilised ------------ (breaks down lactose)

Some people become ill if they consume lactose – they are **lactose intolerant**.

Product out, e.g. -------------------

a. Complete the diagram using words from this list.

amylase   lactase   milk containing lactose   lactose-free milk   starch

[3]

b. The enzyme is **immobilised** in this apparatus. Explain the meaning of the term immobilisation, and suggest why it is important in this process.

Meaning of term ....

Importance .... [2]

Language lab

Fill in the gap.

Plant cells are surrounded by a cell wall. This cell wall is made of ....

1. Pectinase and amylase are enzymes which break down different parts of plant cells. Two students carried out an investigation into the effect of these enzymes on fruit pulp made by crushing oranges in distilled water. The volumes and concentrations of the enzymes were constant. Tubes A, B and C were kept at room temperature (21°C), and tube D was kept at 30°C. The apparatus was left to stand for 24 hours.

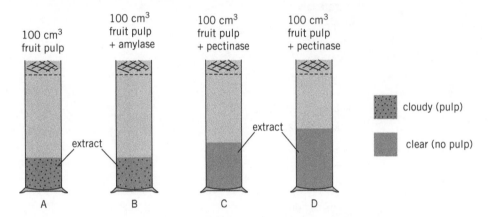

The results are shown in the table below

	A	B	C	D
Volume of extract / cm³	22	23	40	55

a. Calculate the volume of fruit pulp needed to produce 1000 cm³ of clear extract if pectinase is used at room temperature. Show your working.

[3]

b. i. Explain the difference in appearance between tubes B and C.

....

.... [2]

ii. Explain the difference between the results for tubes C and D.

....

.... [2]

c. State the name and action of another enzyme useful in food production.

Name ....

Action .... [2]

132

Language lab

Which one of the following is normally used to produce antibiotics?

A bacteria   B fungi

C protoctists   D viruses

1. a. This graph shows the amounts of *Penicillium* fungus and penicillin in the bioreactor over a period of nine days.

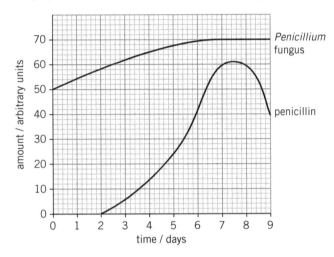

Suggest the best time to collect the penicillin.

....

Explain your answer.

....

.... [2]

b. Doctors are reluctant to prescribe penicillin for all illnesses.

Explain how the overuse of antibiotics can lead to the development of resistant strains of bacteria.

....

....

....

.... [3]

c. Bioreactors may also be used in the production of enzymes.

Complete this table about commercially valuable enzymes. One section has been completed for you.

name of enzyme	commercial value
	clearing fruit juices by digesting clumps of plant cells
lipase from fungi	improves chocolate flow when coating biscuits
	part of biological washing powders – remove blood stains
lactase	

133

A product of genetic engineering, valuable to sufferers from diabetes, is:

A statin   **B** insulin

C amylase   **D** testosterone

1. **a.** The following table gives a list of some terms associated with genetic engineering, and some definitions for these terms.

   Match the terms in column 1 with the correct definition from column 2.

term		definition
gene		a small circle of DNA in a bacterial cell
plasmid		an enzyme that can splice one gene into another section of DNA
vector		an enzyme that can cut out a specific gene from a chromosome
ligase		pieces of single-stranded DNA left exposed after a gene is removed from a chromosome
restriction		a section of DNA coding for a protein
sticky ends		a vessel in which engineered bacteria can produce a valuable product under optimum conditions
fermenter		a structure which can carry a gene into another cell

[6]

   b. Genetic engineering can be used to produce protein products that are useful to humans.

   State **one** reason why each of the following proteins is useful to humans.

   i. Insulin ....

   ....

   ii. Factor 8 ....

   ....

   iii. Pectinase ....

   ....

   iv. Human growth hormone ....

   .... [4]

   c. Before the development of genetic engineering, vaccines were made by heating or chemically treating whole viruses. The vaccine therefore contained whole virus particles.

   Explain why it is safer to use a genetically engineered vaccine rather than one made directly from the hepatitis B virus.

   ....

   ....

   .... [2]

Fill in the gaps.

A .... is a section of .... which codes

for a protein. In animal cells, the .... is carried on long threads called

.... which are found in the .... of the cell.

1. Scientists have found that they can use small rings of DNA called plasmids to transfer useful genes into bacterial cells. The bacterial cells can then manufacture the protein coded for by this gene. The protein can then be extracted from the bacterial cells and may be very valuable in medical treatments for humans.

   The process is outlined in the diagram below.

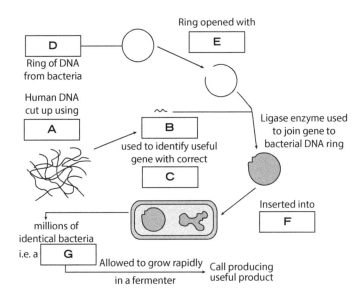

   Match terms from this list with the letters A–G shown on the diagram. [7]

term	letter
plasmid	
restriction enzyme	
gene probe	
sequence of bases	
clone	
protein	
bacterial cell	

Look at the command words section (page 140).

You will see there that you might be asked to define a biological word or term. It is important that you can do this accurately, and without confusion. There are several ways to practise matching words and definitions. Some examples are given below.

Define: the answer is a formal definition of a particular term. The answer is usually 'what is it' – for example, define the term active transport means 'what is active transport'.

Look carefully how many marks are offered. It is often a good idea to add an example to a definition – in this way the examiner can be sure that you know what you are trying to define.

Matching pairs: Organisms and the environment

Use guidelines to match the terms in the first column with the definitions in the second column.

term
food chain
producer
carnivore
trophic level
food web
consumer
herbivore
decomposer
community
population
ecosystem

definition
an organism that gets its energy by feeding on other organisms
a group of organism of one species, living in the same area at the same time
an organism that gets its energy from dead or waste organic material
an animal that gets its energy by eating plants
an animal that gets its energy by eating other animals
the transfer of energy from one organism to the next
an organism that makes its own organic nutrients, usually using energy from sunlight
the position of an organism in a food chain
a unit made up of the community of organisms interacting with their non-living environment
all of the populations of different species in an ecosystem
a network of interconnected food chains

Word scrambles

Read the definition to help unscramble the appropriate word.

Reproduction, menstrual cycle, and pregnancy

UXESAL ODURPCERTONI: Producing new individuals with a combination of features from two parents

MEAGTES: Special sex cells, the sperm and the egg

OYTGEZ: Formed when a sperm and an egg combine

TFIRLISEITOAN: The joining together of sperm and egg

BUPETRY: A stage of human development at which the person becomes able to reproduce

ESX RHOMENOS: Chemicals that control the physical and mental changes at puberty

TEESTS: Where the male gametes are made

ROIEVAS: Where the female gametes are made

IVNAGA: The birth canal

NISEP: Delivers sperm to the vagina

CENPTOICON: The beginning of the development of a new individual

ULPATOIONC: Sexual intercourse – when the sperm from the male are delivered to the female's reproductive system

REYMOB: A stage of development when the ball of cells begins to rearrange itself so that some organs can be seen

STRNAEUTIOMN: The release of the bloody lining of the uterus if no fertilisation has taken place

WGHROT: Getting bigger by the production of more cells

EDLEEOPMVNT: The changes of cells that mean some of them take on different functions

CPLENTAA: A structure linking the umbilical cord to the wall of the uterus

TGATESNIO IPEODR: The length of time between fertilisation and birth

IULIBCALM ROCD: The structure that links the developing fetus to the placenta

INMOATCI IFDUL: Liquid inside a sac that surrounds the developing fetus

**DNA, fingerprints, and forensics
crossword**

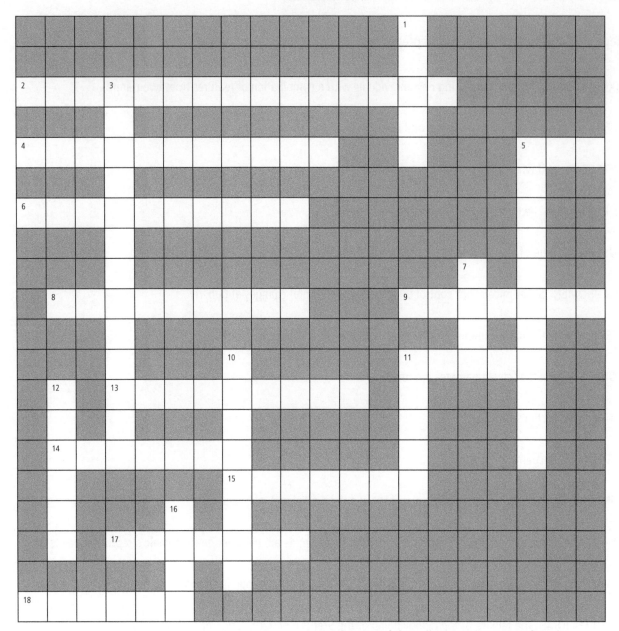

Across:

2 technique for separating DNA fragments on the basis of their size

4 protein found in red blood cells

5 the molecule that carries the information about the function of each cell

6 a subunit of 5 across

8 these people have the same DNA profile (with 11 down: 8,5)

9 the type of molecule which gives a cell its special characteristics

11 the number of bases needed to code for one amino acid in a protein

13 a subunit of a protein (5,4)

14 the base known by the letter T

15 the part of the cell where the DNA is found

17 the partner for 14 across

18 a molecule which can carry out a biological process, such as cutting up DNA into pieces

Down:

1 one of the discoverers of the structure of DNA

3 the scientific word for 'matching' – used to describe base pairs in DNA

5 the shape that the DNA molecule takes up (6,5)

7 the number of different bases found in DNA

10 a branch of science used for the study of criminal activity

11 see 8 across

12 the colleague of 1 down

16 a section of DNA which codes for a single protein

138

Biology involves many words not used in other subjects. Often these words come from Latin or Greek. Some of them will be found in the crossword below.

**Gas exchange
crossword**

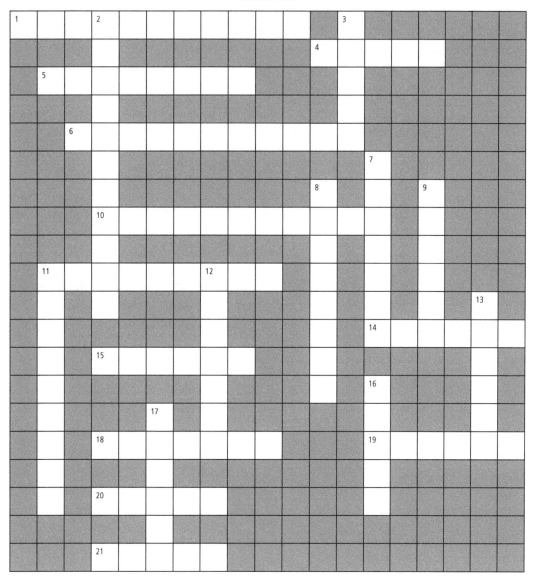

Across:

1 tiny blood vessels
4 secretion which can trap dust in breathing tubes
5 the most abundant gas in the atmosphere
6 fine branches leading to the air sacs
10 a large one is important for gas exchange
11 muscle which separates the abdomen from the thorax – important in quiet breathing
14 the site of exchange of gases
15 gas required for aerobic respiration
18 together with 13 down, a waste product of respiration
19 the voice box (seen as the 'Adam's Apple' in males
20 gas exchange surfaces in fish
21 together with 9 down, there is more of this in exhaled than inhaled air

Down:

2 muscles which contract during forced breathing
3 the organs involved in gas exchange in mammals
7 also known as the windpipe
8 the first branch of 7 down – we have two of them
9 see 21 across
11 process responsible for the movement of oxygen and carbon dioxide
12 another name for 14 across
13 see 18 across
16 tiny hair-like structures which can move dust out of the breathing tubes
17 the type of cell which produces 4 across

Exam success: knowing what to do

Candidates taking an examination in IGCSE Biology are given instructions about what the examiner expects from them. These instructions are given in the introduction to each question, or to each part of a multi-part question. These instructions, which tell the candidate what to do, are given as **command words**.

For example, a candidate might be asked to **define** a biological term, to **describe** a biological process, or to **calculate** a numerical value. Define, describe, and calculate are command words. To be successful in an examination, a candidate must understand what each of the command words means.

Command words: what answer do you expect?

- Command words may require either concise answers or extended answers.

- Command words may require either recall or making logical connections between pieces of information.

- Some command words require only single word or single figure answers.

This list of the command words is taken from the IGCSE syllabus, published by CIE. The examination board stresses that these words are best understood when they are seen in an actual question, and they also point out that some other command words may be used. Even so, this list contains the most commonly used words and what they mean. In other words, these command words tell you what the examiner wants you to do when trying to answer a particular question.

Name: the answer is usually a technical term (diffusion, for example, or mitochondrion) consisting of no more than a few words. **State** is a very similar command word, although the answer may be longer, as a phrase or sentence. **Name** and **state** don't need anything added, i.e. *there is no need for an explanation.* Adding an explanation will take up time and probably won't gain any more marks!

---

a. State **three** normal functions of a root.

1. To anchor the plant in the soil
....

2. To absorb water from the soil
....

3. To absorb mineral ions from the soil
....
[3]

Define: the answer is a formal definition of a particular term. The answer is usually 'what is it' – for example, define the term active transport means 'what is active transport'.

Look carefully at how many marks are offered. It is often a good idea to add an example to a definition – in this way the examiner can be sure that you know what you are trying to define.

What do you understand by or **what is meant by** are commands that also ask for a definition, but again the marks offered suggest that you should add some relevant comment on the importance of the terms concerned.

List: you need to write down a number of points, usually of only one word, with no need for explanation. For example, you might be asked to list four characteristics of living organisms.

Describe: your answer should simply say what is happening in a situation shown in the question, e.g. the number of germinating seeds increased to 55. There is no need for an explanation.

No call for explanation or comment

Make **three** points for the **three** marks on offer

c. (Describe) how water reaches a leaf and enters a palisade cell.

Evaporation/transpiration from leaf surface

water pulled up xylem to replace 'losses'

water moves by osmosis to palisade cell

water crosses palisade cell membrane by osmosis

[3]

d. (Describe) how sugar produced in a palisade cell reaches the roots.

Conversion to sucrose/transported in phloem/

unloaded in roots by diffusion or active transport

[2]

Explain: the answer will be in extended prose, i.e. in the form of complete sentences. You will need to use your knowledge and understanding of biological topics to write more about a statement that has been made in the question, or earlier in your answer.

The command word **explain** is often linked with **describe** or **state**, so that the examiner asks you to **describe and explain** or **state and explain**. This means that there are two parts to be answered – they can often be joined by the word because. For example 'the number of germinating seeds increased to 55 (describe) *because* the temperature has increased and germination is controlled by enzymes which are sensitive to temperature (explain)'.

Many answers fail to gain full marks because they do not obey both commands – they often **describe** but do not **explain**, so only gain half of the available marks.

---

c. There is concern that pollution of the environment may change the breeding grounds of the Adelie penguin.

(State and explain) the effect this might have on the populations of the Leopard seal and the Ross seal.

two pieces of information needed – can you link them with the word 'because'?

Leopard seal Population could fall because there would

be less food for them (so they would breed

less successfully)

Ross seal Population could rise because there would

be fewer leopard seals to act as predators

[4]

Suggest: this command word has two possible meanings. In the first, you will need to use your biological knowledge and understanding to explain something that is new to you. You might use the principle of enzyme action (which you know about) to explain an industrial process (which might be new to you). Suggest also has a second meaning – it implies that that there may be more than one possible answer to a question. For example, there might be a number of different factors affecting the action of a digestive enzyme.

Questions which involve data response (like looking at a table of results, for example) and problem solving (like comparing three different environmental situations, for example) often begin with the command word **suggest**.

Calculate: a numerical answer is expected, usually obtained from data given in the question. Remember:

- show your working (there may be marks given for the correct method even if you get the wrong answer)

- give your answer to the correct number of significant figures, usually two or three

- give the correct units (if needed – sometimes these will already be given in the space left for your answer).

1. The graph below shows the volume of air in the lungs of a person measured over a period of time.

a. i. With reference to the graph calculate, in breaths per minute, the rate of normal breathing between **A** and **B**. (Show your working.)

    3 complete breaths in 12 seconds

    So $3 \times \frac{60}{12}$ breaths in 60 seconds (i.e. 1 minute)

    $= 3 \times 5 = 15$ ......15...... breaths per minute [2]

  Don't forget! You will get a mark for correct working even if you make a mistake with the answer.

ii. State the volume of air remaining in the lungs after the deep breath out.

    1500 cm³

                                              [1]

  Don't forget the units!

iii. (Explain) how the intercostal muscles are involved in breathing from time **B** to time **C**.

    Volume increases because external intercostal muscles

    contract [1 mark] and lift the rib edge upwards

    and outwards [1 mark]

                                              [2]

  *Explain is more than **describe**. Can your answer begin with the word 'because'?*

Other terms which require numerical answers are **find**, **measure**, and **determine**.

Find is a general term, and can mean calculate, measure, or determine.

Measure implies that the answer can be obtained by a direct measurement, e.g. using a ruler to measure the length of a structure on a diagram.

Determine means that the quantity cannot be measured directly, but has to be obtained by calculation or from a graph. For example, the size of a cell from a scale included in the diagram of the cell.

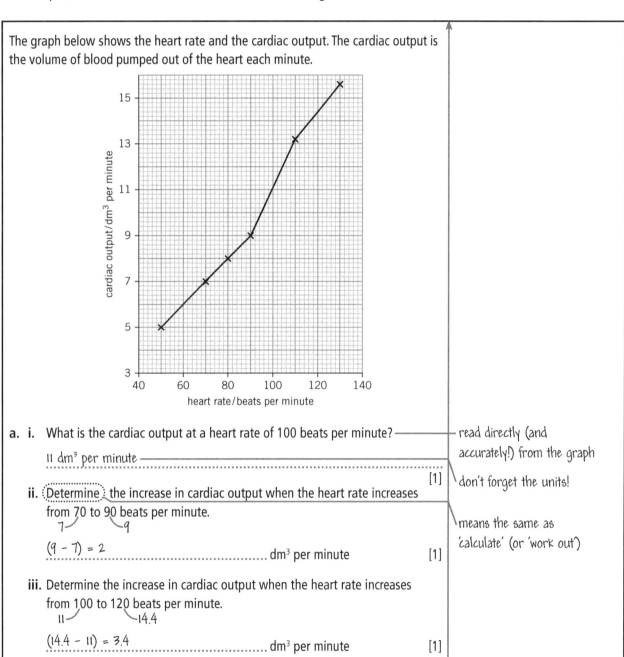

The graph below shows the heart rate and the cardiac output. The cardiac output is the volume of blood pumped out of the heart each minute.

a. i. What is the cardiac output at a heart rate of 100 beats per minute? ———— read directly (and accurately!) from the graph

11 dm³ per minute ————————————————————————————

[1]   don't forget the units!

ii. ⟨Determine⟩ the increase in cardiac output when the heart rate increases from 70 to 90 beats per minute.

    7   9
    (9 − 7) = 2 .... dm³ per minute   [1]

means the same as 'calculate' (or 'work out')

iii. Determine the increase in cardiac output when the heart rate increases from 100 to 120 beats per minute.

    11   14.4
    (14.4 − 11) = 3.4 .... dm³ per minute   [1]

Multiple choice

Remember that there are two alternative multiple-choice papers. Paper 1 contains questions which only assess material from the **core** syllabus; paper 2 contains questions that could contain material from either the **core** or the **supplement**.

Sample 'core' questions

1. Root hair cells are found on plant roots.

   Which of the following features would be present in a root hair cell but not in a cell lining the small intestine?

   A cytoplasm   **B** chloroplasts

   C cell wall   **D** cell membrane

2. Which animal is a spider?

   1. has legs .... go to 2

        has no legs .... go to 3

   2. has six legs .... organism **A**

        has eight legs .... organism **B**

   3. has a shell .... organism **C**

        has no shell .... organism **D**

3. Dietary fibre passes through several structures after leaving the stomach.

   In which order does the dietary fibre pass through these structures?

   A ileum – duodenum – rectum – colon

   B duodenum – ileum – rectum – colon

   C ileum – duodenum – colon – rectum

   D duodenum – ileum – colon – rectum

4. Which chemical elements are found in carbohydrates, fats, and proteins?

	carbohydrates	fats	proteins
A	carbon, hydrogen, and oxygen	carbon, hydrogen, and oxygen	carbon, hydrogen, oxygen, and nitrogen
B	carbon, hydrogen, and oxygen	carbon, hydrogen, oxygen, and nitrogen	carbon, hydrogen, and oxygen
C	carbon, hydrogen, oxygen, and nitrogen	carbon, hydrogen, and oxygen	carbon, hydrogen, and oxygen
D	carbon, hydrogen, oxygen, and nitrogen	carbon, hydrogen, and oxygen	carbon, hydrogen, oxygen, and nitrogen

5. Plant and animal cells have many common structures. State which of the following are present in plant cells but **not** in animal cells.

   A   chloroplast and cell wall

   B   cell membrane and chloroplast

   C   cell membrane and nucleus

   D   nucleus and cell wall

6. The graph shows the effect of light intensity on the rate of photosynthesis at two different temperatures. The concentration of carbon dioxide was kept constant at 0.05%.

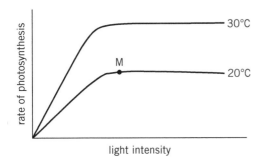

   State which factor is limiting the rate of photosynthesis at point M.

   A   the concentration of carbon dioxide

   B   light intensity

   C   temperature

   D   availability of chlorophyll

7. State which of the following is **not** the result of negative feedback.

   A   a decrease in blood glucose concentration leads to an increase in insulin secretion

   B   an increase in blood glucose concentration leads to an increase in insulin secretion

   C   a decrease in blood glucose concentration leads to a decrease in insulin secretion

   D   an increase in blood glucose concentration leads to an increase in glucagon secretion

8. In a typical reflex action, the relay neurones

   A pass impulses from sensory neurones to motor neurones

   B pass impulses from receptors to motor neurones

   C pass impulses from effectors to motor neurones

   D pass impulses from sensory neurones to effectors

9. A fish has a single circulatory system. State which type of blood leaves the heart of a fish.

   A oxygenated blood at high pressure

   B deoxygenated blood at high pressure

   C oxygenated blood at low pressure

   D deoxygenated blood at low pressure

10.

partially permeable membrane

key:
○ = water molecule
▲ = amino acid molecule

State which arrow

   i. represents osmosis .... [1]

   ii. represents active transport .... [1]

   iii. represents diffusion of amino acids .... [1]

Longer written answers

Remember that there are also two alternative written papers. Paper 3 contains questions that only assess material from the **core** syllabus; paper 4 contains questions that could contain material from either the **core** or the **supplement**.

Sample 'core' questions

11. The diagram below shows the human alimentary canal.

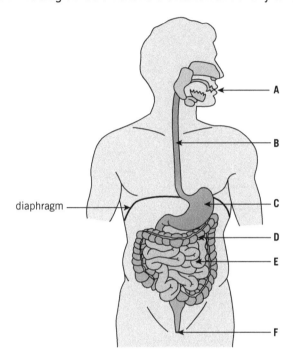

a. On the diagram, draw the liver in the correct place and approximately the right size.   [2]

b. State the name of the process that moves food along the gut.

.... [1]

c. Use the diagram to complete the following table.

Each letter may be used once, more than once, or not at all.

description of site	letter
where saliva is released	
where food is chewed	
where hydrochloric acid is produced	
where soluble foods are absorbed	
where faeces are egested	

[5]

12. The diagram below shows how carbon may be recycled.

The letters represent processes that occur in the cycle.

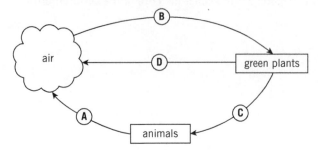

a. i. Use words from the following list to identify the processes **A**, **B**, **C**, and **D**.

feeding   photosynthesis   respiration

The words may be used once, more than once, or not at all.

letter	process
A	
B	
C	
D	

[4]

ii. Name and describe **one** other process which is part of a complete carbon cycle.

....

....

....

.... [3]

b. The diagram below shows a compost heap and the materials used to make it.

   i. Explain why there is a difference in the temperature between the compost heap and the air surrounding it.

   ....

   ....

   .... [2]

   ii. Suggest one reason why a gardener uses an open frame to support the compost heap, rather than close the sides of the frame.

   .... [1]

13. The diagram below shows a section through an air sac and a surrounding blood capillary.

   a. i. List three features shown in the diagram that make an air sac an efficient site for the exchange of gases.

   1. ....

   2. ....

   3. .... [3]

air in and out   wall of alveolus

A

walls of capillary

B

moisture

direction of blood flow

red blood cells

   ii. Suggest why the walls of the air sac contain elastic fibres.

   .... [1]

   b. Use the bar graph to identify **two** differences between the composition of the blood at **A** compared with the composition of the blood at **B**.

   A and **B** are shown in the diagram for part **a**.

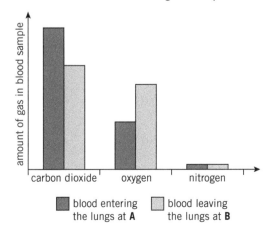

amount of gas in blood sample

carbon dioxide   oxygen   nitrogen

■ blood entering   ☐ blood leaving
the lungs at **A**   the lungs at **B**

1. ....

....

2. ....

.... [2]

c. Suggest **three** ways in which smoking can reduce the efficiency of the lungs.

1. ....

....

2. ....

....

3. ....

.... [3]

14. *In vitro* fertilisation may be helpful to couples who cannot conceive naturally.

This diagram shows the steps in this process

a. Match the structures A, B, C and D with the numbers 1–4 on the diagram

letter A–D	structure	number 1–4
A	Fertilised egg	
B	Embryo	
C	Sperm	
D	Egg	

[3]

b. State the name of the type of cell division responsible for

    i. production of structure 2 .... [1]

    ii. production of structure 4 .... [1]

c. An embryo eventually differentiates into many different types of cell, forming tissues, organs, and organ systems in an organism.

    i. State the name of the type of cell **in an adult** which retains the power to differentiate into several different tissues .... [1]

    ii. Suggest one site where this type of cell might be found in an adult human .... [1]

15. Phenyketonuria is an inherited disease. The allele for the disease (p) is recessive to the normal allele (P). The diagram below shows the inheritance of PKU in three generations of one family.

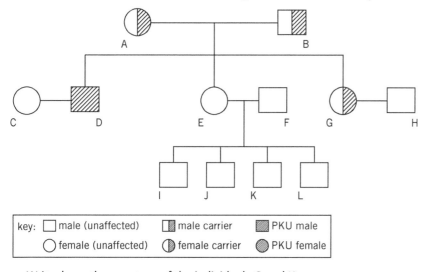

a. Write down the genotype of the individuals G and K

    G..   K..   [2]

b. State how many of the children of the couple A and B are homozygous .... [1]

c. If C and D have a child, what is the probability that the child will have PKU?

    .... [1]

d. E and F have four children. All are male. What is the probability that their next child will be male?

    .... [1]

Sample 'supplement' questions

16.a. The following sentences describe the feeding relationships between four organisms.

    Owls obtain some of their energy from thrushes

    Apple moth caterpillars are herbivores.

    An apple tree carries out photosynthesis.

    Thrushes are secondary consumers.

    i. Write out a food chain containing these four organisms.

    [3]

ii. State the main source of energy for the food chain

.... [1]

b. A group of students studied all of the organisms in an orchard of apple trees. They estimated the biomass of the different organisms.

The students divided the organisms into four groups according to their positions in the food web. Their results are shown in the table. Detritivores are animals that feed on parts of dead organisms.

position of organisms in the food web	biomass / g per m² of orchard
Producers	280
Herbivores	105
Detritivores	90
Carnivores	25

i. Use the information in the table to complete a pyramid of biomass on the grid. The scientists observed the detritivores feeding on dead plants, so decided to count herbivores and detritivores as one group of organisms.

(subdivide sectors into tens on grid)

ii. Define the term **trophic level**. ....

.... [1]

iii. Explain why there are very rarely more than four or five trophic levels in an ecosystem.

....

....

.... [2]

iv. The scientists obtained records of animal numbers over a period of years. They noticed that the number of owls was falling, and classified the owls as 'endangered'.

A species becomes endangered when it is at danger of extinction.

Suggest **two** ways in which an animal could become endangered.

....

....

.... [2]

v. Suggest **one** way in which endangered species can be conserved.

....

....

.... [2]

17. A doctor asked a patient to look carefully at the food labels of each item she ate during one day, and to note down

i. the different foods she ate

ii. the salt content of each food

iii. what proportion of the recommended daily amount (RDA) of salt to which this was equivalent.

a. Suggest why too much salt in the diet can be harmful. ....

.... [1]

b. The results she obtained are shown in this table.

food	amount of salt in food / g	% of RDA of salt
Breakfast cereal	0.2	3.3
Toast and butter	0.9	15.0
Tinned pasta	2.0	33.0
Tin of vegetable soup	2.5	41.7
Tinned beans	0.7	11.7
Ketchup	0.5	8.2
Chicken pie	1.3	21.7

i. State the range for the amount of salt in the different foods. .... [2]

ii. The RDA for salt is 6.0g. Calculate how much more than the RDA of salt the patient ate.

.... [2]

c. As well as salt, some other foods are essential in small quantities. Suggest which of the foods in the above list would provide most vitamin D.

.... [1]

In the design of an experiment, a variable is a factor which can be changed.

1. A student carrying out food tests for biological molecules had seen on the internet that **cow's milk contained more sugar than soya milk**. He suggested that the group should test this hypothesis.

    a. Describe how you would carry out the test for a simple sugar.

    ....

    ....

    .... [3]

    b. The test would only be valuable if it is **quantitative**. State the meaning of the term quantitative.

    .... [1]

    c. The teacher suggested that the students should fill in this table, to make sure that they had a plan that would provide them with valid data. Complete the table.

Which variable would you change in the experiment? This is the **independent variable**.	
Which three variables would you keep the same? These are the **fixed variables**.	
Which variable would you measure to test the hypothesis? This is the **dependent variable**.	
How would you measure this variable?	
Suggest a control for the experiment.	
Suggest why you would repeat the experiment.	

[8]

Absorption: Movement of small food molecules and ions through the wall of the intestine into the blood or lymph.

Accommodation: The adjustment of the shape of the lens to accurately focus light onto the retina.

Active immunity: Defence against a pathogen, or response to a vaccine, by antibody production in the body.

Active transport: The movement of particles from a region of lower concentration to one of higher concentration, across a membrane, using energy from respiration.

Adaptive feature: An inherited feature that helps an organism to survive and reproduce in its environment.

Adrenaline: Hormone produced by the adrenal glands and prepares the body for stress – the 'fright, flight or fight' hormone.

Aerobic respiration: The chemical reactions in cells that use oxygen to break down food molecules and release a relatively large amount of energy.

AIDS: The weakening of the body's immune system, following infection by HIV.

Allele: An alternative form of a gene (a gene may have two or more alleles).

Amino acid: A sub-unit of a protein.

Amylase: The enzyme that digests starch to maltose.

Anaerobic respiration: The chemical reactions in cells that break down food molecules in the absence of oxygen and release a relatively small amount of energy.

Anaemia: An inability of the red blood cells to carry oxygen. Caused by faulty haemoglobin, and leads to weakness.

Anther: A male part of a flower, where pollen grains are produced.

Antibiotic: A drug (penicillin, for example) which slows the growth of, or kills, bacteria in the body.

Antibody: A protein released by lymphocytes which can recognise and bind to antigens.

Antigen: A molecule, often part of a pathogen, which can be recognised by the immune system.

Antiseptic: A substance which kills bacteria outside the body, on a kitchen surface for example.

Artery: A blood vessel which carries blood away from the heart.

Arthropod: An animal with jointed legs and a hard exoskeleton.

Artificial insemination (AI): Placing semen into the uterus as means of increasing fertility.

Artificial selection: The choice of animals or plants for breeding because they have characteristics useful to humans, e.g. a high yield of milk.

Asexual reproduction: Reproduction without the involvement of gametes or zygotes so that offspring are genetically identical to their parents.

Assimilation: The use of digested food molecules by cells, e.g. the synthesis of proteins from amino acids.

Atrium: A chamber of the heart that receives blood from veins and pumps it through to a ventricle.

Auxin: A plant growth hormone which is involved in tropic responses as it controls cell elongation.

Bacterium: Microorganism with cells that have cytoplasm and a cell wall, but no distinct nucleus. A prokaryote.

Balanced diet: A diet that provides carbohydrates, fats, proteins, vitamins, minerals, water, and fibre in the correct proportions.

Bile: An alkaline fluid made in the liver and stored in the gall bladder. Bile is important in emulsification of fats in the small intestine and in the creation of an alkaline pH for the action of digestive enzymes there.

Binary fission: Asexual reproduction in which one cell divides into two, then two into four and so on.

Binomial system: Naming species in a system in which the scientific name of an organism is made up of two parts, showing the genus and the species. Humans, for example, have the binomial name *Homo sapiens*.

Biodegradable: Material that can be broken down by biological processes, usually involving microorganisms.

Biodiversity: The number and variety of living organisms.

Biomass: The mass of material, in a given area, derived from living organisms.

Biotechnology: The use of living organisms to carry out processes useful to humans, such as producing medicines or degrading wastes.

Blind spot: Part of the retina where the optic nerve leaves the eyeball so there are no photoreceptors.

Capillary: The smallest blood vessel, joining arteries to veins. The capillary is the site of exchange between blood and tissue fluid and has walls only one cell thick.

Cancer: Uncontrolled cell division leading to disease.

Carbohydrate: A class of molecule, containing carbon, hydrogen, and oxygen, and a major source of energy in food. Examples are starch and glucose.

Carnivore: An animal that gets its energy and raw materials by eating other animals.

Carrier: In genetics, an individual heterozygous for a recessive allele. The allele is not expressed but can be 'carried' to the next generation.

Catalyst: A substance that increases the rate of a chemical reaction and is not changed by the reaction.

Cellulose: An insoluble carbohydrate that makes up the cell wall of plant cells.

Central nervous system (CNS): The brain and spinal cord.

Chemical digestion: Breakdown of large, insoluble food molecules into small soluble ones. The process usually involves enzymes.

Chlorophyll: The green pigment, found within the chloroplast of plant cells, which absorbs light energy for photosynthesis.

Chloroplast: Organelle in plant cells that contains chlorophyll and carries out photosynthesis.

Cholera: A disease of the intestines in which water reabsorption is affected. Caused by a bacterium, *Vibrio cholerae*.

Cholesterol: A lipid-like molecule which is linked to higher risks of atherosclerosis and heart disease.

Chromosome: A thread-like structure of DNA, carrying genetic information in the form of genes.

Clone: A group of genetically identical organisms. Usually formed by mitosis.

Clotting: A series of processes that cause blood cells and fragments to clump together and seal damaged blood vessels.

Codominance: The existence of two alleles of a gene where neither is dominant over the other, and both are expressed in the heterozygote. The alleles I^A and I^B for blood groups are an example.

Community: All of the populations of different species in an ecosystem.

Competition: The situation in which different organisms are seeking the same resource, such as food or nesting sites.

Concentration gradient: The difference in concentration of a solute between two different places.

Conservation: Work carried out by humans to protect species and maintain biodiversity, or to maintain a supply of limited resources.

Consumer: An organism that gets its energy by feeding on other organisms.

Continuous variation: Differences between organisms that show a range of phenotypes between extremes with many intermediates. Often results from effects of both genes and the environment.

Coronary heart disease (CHD): Disease of the heart caused by blockage of the coronary arteries. Risk is increased by fatty diets and poor exercise habits.

Cross pollination: Transfer of pollen grains from the anther of one flower to the stigma on a different plant of the same species.

Cystic fibrosis: Disease of the lungs and digestive system caused by excessive secretion of sticky mucus. Results from a mutant recessive allele so is only expressed in homozygous individuals.

Deamination: The removal of the nitrogen-containing part of amino acids to form urea.

Decomposer: An organism that gets its energy from dead or waste organic material.

Deforestation: The removal of trees by humans to clear land for agriculture or for building.

Denitrification: Conversion of nitrate to nitrogen by bacteria, as part of the nitrogen cycle.

Development: The increase in complexity of an organism as it grows and produces new tissues, organs, and systems.

Diabetes: A medical condition in which the blood glucose concentration is not controlled. Can be caused by failure of the pancreas to secrete insulin or by a diet high in sugars.

DCPIP: A chemical which can be used to measure the concentration of vitamin C in a solution, as it is decolourised from blue to colourless.

Diffusion: The net movement of particles from a region of higher concentration to one of lower concentration. The particles move down a concentration gradient as their kinetic energy results in their random movement.

Digestion: The breakdown of large, insoluble molecules into smaller, soluble molecules using chemical and mechanical processes.

Diploid nucleus: A nucleus containing two sets of chromosomes, usually in pairs. Present in most body cells.

Discontinuous variation: Few phenotypes for a particular characteristic, with no intermediate forms. Typically the result of genes alone.

DNA: The molecule that forms the genetic material. Genetic information is stored as a sequence of bases in the DNA.

Dominant: An allele that is expressed if it is present in a heterozygote.

Drug: Any substance taken into the body that modifies or affects chemical reactions in the body.

Ecosystem: A unit containing the community of living organisms interacting with their physical environment.

Egestion: The passing out of food that has not been digested or absorbed, as faeces through the anus.

Embryo: The early stage of a plant or animal as it grows and develops by mitosis from a fertilised egg.

Emphysema: A lung disease in which the walls of the air sacs are broken down and so lose their ability to transfer oxygen and carbon dioxide between blood and air.

Emulsification: The breakdown of large fat globules into many smaller ones, in the presence of bile.

Enzymes: Proteins that function as biological catalysts.

Eutrophication: The effect of nitrates and phosphates on the growth of algae and aquatic plants. Can lead to a decrease in the oxygen content of water, and death of aerobic organisms.

Evolution: The process in which inherited features of organisms change over a period of time.

Excretion: Removal of toxic materials, waste products of metabolism and substances in excess of the body's requirements.

Extinction: The loss of a species from the Earth's community.

Fats: Lipids that are insoluble in water and contain three fatty acids linked to a glycerol molecule. Important as energy stores and in thermal insulation.

Fermentation: A form of anaerobic respiration in which glucose is converted to carbon dioxide and alcohol. The term is also used to describe industrial processes in which microorganisms make products useful to humans.

Fermenter: A large container where microorganisms can be grown under controlled conditions to make useful products. Also called a bioreactor.

Fertilisation: The fusion of male and female gametes to produce a zygote.

Fertiliser: Plant nutrients that can be used to stimulate plant growth. Usually contain nitrate, phosphate, and, often, potassium.

Fetus: A stage during the development of a mammal when all the major organs are present.

Fibre: Indigestible plant material that helps the action of the alimentary canal and the formation of faeces.

Food chain: The transfer of energy from one organism to the next, beginning with the absorption of light energy by a producer.

Food web: A network of interconnected food chains.

Gall bladder: A sac in the liver which stores bile before its release into the small intestine.

Gametes: Sex cells with the haploid number of chromosomes e.g. sperm and egg in animals.

Gene: A length of DNA that codes for a protein.

Gene mutation: A change in the base sequence of DNA.

Genetic engineering: Changing the genetic material of an organism by removing, changing or inserting individual genes.

Genotype: The genetic make-up of an organism in terms of the genes present.

Genus: A unit of classification containing a group of species with similar characteristics.

Glucagon: Hormone produced by the pancreas that helps to increase blood glucose concentration by stimulating the liver to convert glycogen to glucose.

Glycogen: An insoluble carbohydrate used as an energy store in animal cells, usually in the liver and muscles.

Gravtitropism: A response in which parts of a plant grow towards (positive) or away from (negative) gravity.

Greenhouse effect: Keeping the Earth's surface warm as greenhouse gases, especially carbon dioxide and methane, reduce the loss of heat energy through the atmosphere. Occurs naturally but is becoming more extreme (enhanced) by emissions resulting from human activity.

Growth: A permanent increase in size and dry mass by an increase in cell size and/or cell number.

Haemoglobin: The red pigment in red blood cells. Contains iron, and combines with oxygen so that the red cells can carry this gas.

Haploid nucleus: A nucleus containing a single set of unpaired chromosomes, e.g. in gametes.

Herbivore: An animal that obtains its energy and raw materials by eating plants.

Heterozygous: Having two different alleles of a particular gene.

HIV (Human Immunodeficiency Virus): The virus that attacks lymphocytes and so reduces the efficiency of the human immune system, leading to AIDS.

Homeostasis: The maintenance of a constant internal environment.

Homologous chromosomes: A pair of matching chromosomes that carry genes for the same characteristic in the same positions.

Homozygous: Having two identical alleles of a particular gene.

Hormone: A chemical substance produced by a gland and carried in the blood and alters the activity of one or more specific target organs.

Immunity: Protection against infection by pathogens using antibodies and cells such as phagocytes.

Implantation: The embedding of an embryo into the wall of the uterus at the start of the gestation period in mammals.

Ingestion: The taking in of substances into the body through the mouth.

Inheritance: The transmission of genetic information from generation to generation.

Insulin: Hormone secreted by the pancreas which reduces the blood glucose concentration.

***In vitro* fertilisation (IVF):** The mixing of sperm and eggs in a dish outside the body. The gametes fuse at fertilisation and the resulting embryo is inserted into the uterus.

Iris: A ring of muscle which controls the entry of light into the eye and so can protect the retina from over-stimulation.

Lactase: Enzyme which breaks down milk sugar (lactose). Can be immobilised for use in the preparation of lactose-free milk.

Lacteal: Structure inside the villus which transports absorbed fats away from the intestine.

Lactic acid: A product of anaerobic respiration in animals.

Lens: A structure responsible for the fine focussing of light on the retina.

Limiting factor: Something present in the environment in such short supply that it restricts life processes, e.g. light intensity may be the limiting factor that limits the rate of photosynthesis.

Ligase: An enzyme used in genetic engineering used to stitch together two pieces of DNA, such as a plasmid and an opened chromosome.

Lipase: Enzyme which digests fats to fatty acids and glycerol.

Liver: Organ which carries out many of the reactions of metabolism, including production of bile and deamination of excess amino acids.

Malnutrition: Condition caused by eating an unbalanced diet. Can be undernutrition when the diet is deficient in some way, or overnutrition when some part of the diet is present in excess.

Mechanical digestion: The physical breakdown of food into smaller pieces, without the involvement of enzymes, e.g. by chewing with teeth.

Meiosis: Division of the nucleus to produce cells (gametes) with half of the normal chromosome number. The gametes also contain different combinations of genetic material.

Memory cells: Cells produced as a result of exposure to an antigen, for example in a vaccine, so that the body is prepared for further infection by the same antigen.

Menstruation: The breakdown of the lining of the uterus as part of the menstrual cycle so that blood and cells are discharged through the vagina.

Metabolism: The sum of the chemical reactions occurring in cells.

Mitochondrion: Organelle which carries out aerobic respiration and so provides energy for metabolism.

Mitosis: Division of the nucleus which produces genetically identical cells with the same chromosome number as the parent cells.

Motor neurone: Nerve cell which carries impulses from the CNS to an effector such as a muscle.

Movement: An action causing a change in position of an organism or part of an organism.

Mutation: A change in the genetic material of an organism. Occurs naturally but rate can be increased by radiation or by some chemicals.

Natural selection: The effect of the environment on the survival of individuals so that different individuals are able to pass on their genetic material to successive generations.

Negative feedback: The mechanism for maintaining homeostasis in which a change from the optimum conditions causes a response to cancel out the change.

Nitrification: Conversion of ammonium ions to nitrate, as part of the nitrogen cycle.

Nitrogen fixation: Conversion of nitrogen gas to nitrogen-containing compounds. Often carried out by bacteria in nodules on the roots of legumes.

Nucleus: Control centre of the cell, contains the chromosomes.

Nutrition: The taking in of materials for energy, growth, and development.

Obesity: A body mass which is greater than that recommended for good health. May be caused by overnutrition, where energy consumed is greatly in excess of energy needs.

Oestrogen: Hormone responsible for development of female secondary sexual characteristics.

Organ: A structure made of a group of different tissues working together to perform a specific function.

Organ system: A group of organs working together to perform a specific function in the body, e.g. stomach, ileum, colon, and rectum in the digestive system.

Osmosis: The net movement of water molecules from a region of higher water potential to one of lower water potential, through a partially permeable membrane.

Ovule: The structure inside the ovary of a plant that contains the female gamete. After fertilisation the ovule develops into a seed.

Ovum: Female sex cell (gamete), produced in the ovary.

Oxygen debt: The extra oxygen 'owed' to the body to respire lactic acid produced during anaerobic respiration in animals.

Pancreas: The organ which (a) produces insulin and glucagon to regulate blood glucose concentration and (b) produces digestive enzymes active in the small intestine.

Partially permeable membrane: A membrane, such as the cell membrane, that allows some particles to pass through but prevents the passage of others. Sometimes called a selectively permeable membrane.

Passive immunity: Short-term defence against a pathogen by antibodies provided by another individual, e.g. from mother to infant in breast milk.

Pathogen: A disease-causing organism.

Pectinase: An enzyme that breaks down plant cell walls and can be used for 'clearing' fruit juices.

Pesticide: A chemical that kills pests (a pest is an organism that competes with humans for resources).

Phagocyte: A type of white blood cell that ingests and digest pathogens as part of an immune response.

Phenotype: The observable features of an organism; affected by both genes and environment.

Phloem: Plant tissue which transports the products of photosynthesis such as sucrose.

Photosynthesis: The process by which plants manufacture carbohydrates from carbon dioxide and water, using energy from light.

Phototropism: A response in which parts of a plant grow towards (positive) or away from (negative) the direction from which light is coming.

Plasma: The liquid part of blood, responsible for transporting many solutes such as dissolved foods, urea and hormones.

Plasmid: A small ring of DNA found in bacterial cells and useful as a vector in genetic engineering.

Platelets: Small fragments of red blood cells used in the blood clotting process.

Pollination: Transfer of pollen grains from anther to stigma, of the same or a different plant.

Population: A group of organisms of a single species living in the same area at the same time.

Producer: An organism that makes its own organic nutrients, usually using energy from sunlight, by photosynthesis.

Prokaryote: A cell without its DNA contained inside a clear nucleus.

Protease: Enzyme which digests protein to amino acids.

Protein: Large molecule composed of amino acids linked by peptide bonds.

Protoctist: Microscopic single-celled organism which may have some animal features (e.g. *Amoeba*) or some plant features (e.g. *Euglena*).

Puberty: The stage of development at which secondary sexual characteristics appear.

Pulse: An expansion of the elastic wall of an artery as blood is forced out from the left ventricle of the heart.

Pyramid of biomass: An illustration of the amount of biomass at each trophic level in an ecosystem.

Pyramid of numbers: An illustration of the number of organisms at each trophic level in an ecosystem.

Receptor: Cell which can receive a stimulus and then produce an impulse.

Recessive: One of a pair of alleles that is only expressed when in the homozygous condition.

Recycling: Conversion of waste material back to a form in which it can be useful to humans.

Red blood cell: Cell which transports oxygen from lung to tissues.

Reflex action: An automatic response to a given stimulus, which often has a survival value.

Relay neurone: A nerve cell within the CNS which transfers impulses from a sensory neurone to a motor neurone.

Reproduction: The process that make more of the same kind of organism.

Respiration: The chemical processes in the cell that break down nutrient molecules to release energy for metabolism.

Response: An action carried out by an effector as a result of a particular stimulus.

Restriction enzyme: An enzyme used in genetic engineering to cut DNA at specific places.

Retina: The light-sensitive layer of the eye, containing the photoreceptors rods and cones.

Ribosome: Organelle which can synthesise proteins from amino acids.

Root hair: Specialised cell in a root that provides a large surface area for the absorption of water and mineral ions.

Rough endoplasmic reticulum: A network of membranes inside cells with ribosomes attached for the efficient synthesis of proteins from amino acids.

Secretion: The release of a useful product from a cell, e.g. mucus from goblet cells in the bronchi.

Selective breeding: The choice of animals or plants for breeding because they have characteristics useful to humans, e.g. a high yield of milk.

Self pollination: The transfer of pollen from the anther to the stigma of the same flower.

Sense organ: A collection of receptor cells sensitive to the same stimulus, e.g. the eye is a sense organ sensitive to light.

Sensitivity: The ability to detect and respond to changes in the environment.

Sensory neurone: Nerve cell which carries impulses from a receptor to the CNS.

Sex chromosomes: A pair of chromosomes which determine the sex of an individual, e.g. in humans XX is female and XY is male.

Sex-linked characteristic: A characteristic for which the gene responsible is located on a sex chromosome, usually the X chromosome.

Sexual reproduction: A process involving the fusion of the nuclei of two gametes (sex cells) to form a zygote, and the formation of offspring that are genetically different from one another and from their parents.

Sexually transmitted infection (STI): An infection that is transmitted in body fluids through sexual contact.

Species: A group of animals with so many similar characteristics that they are capable of interbreeding and producing fertile offspring.

Sperm: Male sex cell (gamete) produced in the testes.

Starch: An insoluble carbohydrate often used as an energy store in plant cells.

Stem cells: Unspecialised cells that multiply by mitosis and then can become specialised to form a range of different tissues, e.g. cells in the bone marrow can become different types of blood cell.

Stimulus: A change in the environment that can be detected by a receptor.

Stoma (plural: stomata): A small gap in the epidermis of a leaf that allows gases to diffuse in and out. The size of the gap is controlled by guard cells.

Sustainable development: Development providing resources for an increasing human population without changing the environment to make it unsuitable for future generations.

Sustainable resource: One that is produced as rapidly as it is removed from the environment so that it does not run out, e.g. timber from managed forests.

Synapse: A junction between two neurones.

Test cross: A genetic cross which crosses a known genotype (a homozygous recessive) with another organism in order to work out the unknown genotype.

Testosterone: Male sex hormone, produced in the testes, responsible for the development of male secondary sexual characteristics.

Tissue: A group of cells with similar structures working together to carry out a particular function.

Translocation: The movement of the products of photosynthesis, sucrose and amino acids, through the phloem.

Transmissible disease: A disease in which the pathogen can be passed from one host to another.

Transpiration: Loss of water by plant leaves by evaporation and diffusion.

Trophic level: The position of an organism in a food chain, food web, pyramid of numbers, or pyramid of biomass.

Tropism: A growth response of part of a plant to an external stimulus, such as light or gravity.

Turgor: A pressure inside a plant cell caused by the cytoplasm pushing against the cellulose cell wall.

Urea: A waste product produced by deamination of amino acids in the liver. It is expelled from the blood as urine from the kidneys.

Urine: An excretory fluid formed in the kidneys by filtration of the blood. It contains urea, salts, and variable amounts of water.

Uterus: A muscular chamber in the female where an implanted embryo develops into a fetus during the gestation period. Also known as the womb.

Vaccine: A product containing a mild or killed pathogen to stimulate the activity of the immune system and so provide protection against a disease.

Vaccination: The process of delivering a vaccine to provide immunity.

Vacuole: A fluid-filled sac present in most plant cells but very rarely in animal cells.

Vagina: A muscular tube leading from the uterus to the outside which acts as the birth canal.

Variation: Differences between individuals of the same species – may be continuous or discontinuous.

Vasoconstriction: Reduction in the diameter of blood vessels, especially in the skin when conserving heat.

Vasodilation: Increase in the diameter of blood vessels, especially in the skin when trying to lose heat.

Vein: Blood vessel which returns blood towards the heart, often with the help of flap-like valves.

Ventricle: Lower chamber of the heart, which is muscular to expel blood into the arteries.

Vertebrate: An animal with a backbone.

Villus: A structure which increases the surface area of the small intestine to increase the surface area for absorption of digested food molecules.

Virus: A microscopic organism, containing nucleic acid surrounded by a protein coat, and which can only reproduce inside a living cell.

Vitamin: A nutrient needed in very small amounts but which is essential to aid the use of other nutrients.

Water potential: The tendency for water molecules to move by diffusion, i.e. down a gradient of water potential.

White blood cells: Cells which are usually involved with defence against disease or infection. Includes lymphocytes and phagocytes.

Wilting: Drooping of plants as water loss causes a loss of turgor in the plant cells.

Xerophyte: A plant adapted to life in very dry environments.

Xylem: The tissue in a plant through which water and minerals are transported.

Yeast: A single-celled fungus that is widely used in biotechnology as it converts glucose to alcohol and carbon dioxide.

Zygote: The product of fertilisation i.e. the fusion of male and female gametes.

Unit 1.1
LL true
1. A: sensitivity; B: reproduction; C: excretion; D: respiration
2. C
3. kingdom – phylum – class – order – family – genus – species

Unit 1.2
LL mammalia; genus; species
1. a. i. *Parus caeruleus* and *Parus major*; they belong to the same genus
   b. i.
E. rubecula	X	X	X
P. caeruleus	X	✓	✓
P. major	X	✓	✓
T. merula	✓	X	X
      ii. Pale area only below eye *Parus major*
          Pale areas above and below eye *Parus caeruleus*

Unit 1.3
LL Literal meaning is 'before nucleus', and refers to the absence of a nuclear membrane in these organisms
1. a. i. chloroplast   ii. nutrition (photosynthesis)
   b. i. excretion   ii. movement
   c. respiration

Unit 1.4
LL vertebrates; classes; mammals; reptiles; fish
1. a. An animal with a backbone
   b. scales; no; no; yes; fur; yes

Unit 1.5
LL 1. false 2. false 3. true 4. false
1. a. ant: three/yes; earthworm: none/no; centipede: many/yes; mite: four/no
   b. ant – insect; earthworm – annelid; centipede – myriapod; mite – arachnid

Unit 1.6
LL stem; leaves; cellulose; ferns
1. a. stem – hold leaves in best position; roots – absorb water and mineral ions; leaves – trap light energy for photosynthesis; flowers – may be attractive to pollinating insects or birds; fruit – usually help dispersal of seed, a reproductive structure
   b. chlorophyll   autotrophic   photosynthesis   cellulose   ferns   angiosperms   monocotyledons   dicotyledons

Unit 1.7
LL true
1. A: *Thynnus*   B: *Exocoetus*   C: *Paracirrhites*   D: *Scyliorhinus*

Unit 2.1
1. a. 10
   b. 1000
2. a. A – cell surface membrane; B – cytoplasm; C – nucleus
   b. nucleus
   c. cellulose cell wall/chloroplast/permanent vacuole
   d. 3 mm = 3000 μm   Magnification $= \frac{3000}{25} = \times 120$

Unit 2.2
LL Plant cells have a rigid cellulose cell wall, which fixes their shape. Animal cells have only a flexible cell surface membrane.
1. a. A: nucleus;   B: chloroplast
   b. i. show a granule (mitochondrion) in the cytoplasm
      ii. mitochondrion
   c. Measured diameter = 3 cm = 30 000 μm
      Actual diameter = 25 μm
      Magnification $= \frac{30\,000}{25} = 1200$
   d. partially/differentially permeable membrane

Unit 2.3
LL nucleus – site of DNA; ribosome – protein synthesis; mitochondrion – respiration; cell membrane – active transport

1. a. i. Could label nucleus/cell membrane/cytoplasm
      ii. chloroplast
      iii. cellulose cell wall/permanent vacuole
   b. i. mitochondria
      ii. ribosomes (accept rough endoplasmic reticulum)

Unit 2.4
LL red blood cell – oxygen transport; neurone – impulse conduction; phloem sieve tube – sucrose transport; root hair cell – ion uptake
1. a. From top line, reading right to left:
      cell C, 1, 2, 3; cell B, 1, 2, 3; cell F, 1, 4, 5, 6, 7; cell I, 1, 4, 5, 8; cell E, 1, 4, 5, 6; cell A, 1, 2; cell H, 1, 4, 5, 8; cell D, 1, 4; cell G, 1, 4, 5, 6, 7
   b. leaf

Unit 2.5
LL D: tissues – organs – systems
1. a. heart – circulatory;   stomach – digestive;   bladder – urinary/excretory
   b. phloem – transport; stamens – reproductive
2. a. i. B   ii. D
   b. bone marrow

Unit 3.1
LL It is partially correct – diffusion does NOT need the presence of a partially permeable membrane
1. Diffusion; down; gas; random; equilibrium;
   Osmosis; diffusion; potential; partially permeable
2. **Movement of materials crossword**
   Across:
   1. membrane
   7. active transport
   10. potential
   11. osmosis
   12. carrier
   Down:
   1. metabolism
   2. water
   3. diffusion
   4. gradient
   5. energy
   6. solute
   8. oxygen
   9. glucose

Unit 3.2
LL diffusion; water; partially permeable membrane; flaccid; turgid
1. a. i. +8, +4, −1, −6, −10
      ii. graph plotted
      iii. 0.45
      iv. Represents an equilibrium so shows water potential of cell cytoplasm
   b. osmosis

Unit 3.3
LL flaccid; osmosis; cellulose; lysis
1. a. Rigid due to hydrostatic pressure against inside of cellulose cell wall
   b. Offers support – diagram should show protoplast pushing against inside of cellulose cell wall
   c. i. A
      ii. The potato chip would straighten/become rigid as water would enter (down the water potential gradient) by osmosis

Unit 3.4
LL C and D are true
1. a. i. B   ii. C
   b. D
   c. Movement is against a concentration gradient
   d. 1. Mineral ion, e.g. magnesium ion, into root hair
      2. Glucose/amino acids from gut contents across villi into bloodstream

Unit 4.1
LL True
1. a. glucose; cellulose; sucrose; soluble
   b. fatty acids; glycerol; insoluble
   c. haemoglobin; amino acids; soluble
   d. DNA
2. a. i. vitamin C   ii. blue to colourless
   b. orange juice

Unit 4.2

LL protein – enzymes are examples; fat – are insoluble in water; carbohydrate – contain approximately twice as many hydrogen atoms as oxygen atoms; vitamin C – can oxidise DCPIP

1. **a.** **i.** higher protein content
        ii. Earlier step in food chain, so more can be produced per unit area.
    b. **i.** sample Z
        ii. as a reagent blank
        iii. sample X

Unit 5.1

LL 1 – true; 2 – false; 3 – false

1. protein – the type of molecule that makes up an enzyme; substrate – a molecule that reacts in an enzyme-catalysed reaction; product – the molecule made in an enzyme-catalysed reaction; active site – the part of the enzyme where substrate molecules can bind; denaturation – a change in shape of an enzyme so that its active site cannot bind to the substrate; optimum – the ideal value of a factor, such as temperature, for an enzyme to work
2. lipase; cuts out useful genes from chromosomes; removes milk sugar from milk; protease; cellulase; amylase

Unit 5.4

LL 1 – true; 2 – false; 3 – true

1. **a** temperature on *x* axis, time taken on *y* axis
    b. 35°C
    c. these are fixed variables
    d. Enzyme is denatured – loss of active site so cannot have binding of substrate to enzyme
    e. pH/enzyme concentration/substrate concentration

Unit 5.5

LL The loss of the three-dimensional structure of an enzyme (particularly its active site), usually caused by extremes of temperature or pH

1. **a.** Check correct column headings, e.g. temperature (°C) and time for clotting (minutes)
    b. Graph plotted – temperature on *x* axis
    c. 45 °C
    d. **i.** pH
        ii. use buffer solutions

Unit 5.6

LL optimum; stomach; duodenum/ileum/small intestine

1. **a.** **i.** amino acids/peptides   **ii.** 54 mg
    b. **i.** 7.0/8.0   **ii.** 2.4
    c. Hydrochloric acid is added from cells lining the glands of the stomach
    d. **i.** lipase
        ii. fatty acids and glycerol
        iii. bile; by breaking it down to fat droplets (emulsification) increases surface area for action of lipase

Unit 6.1

LL water; glucose

1. photosynthesis; light/solar; chloroplasts/chlorophyll; carbon dioxide; water; starch; oxygen; stomata
2. **a.** carbon dioxide
    b. oxygen
    c. water
    d. nitrate
    e. magnesium

Unit 6.2

LL starch; iodine; brown; blue-black

1. **a.** to destarch it (remove any starch already present)
    b. magnesium
    c. chlorophyll (necessary to absorb light energy) or light energy (needed to split water to begin production of carbohydrate)

Unit 6.3

LL 1 – false; 2 – true

1. **a.** starch
    b./ c. Starch gives a blue-black colour with iodine solution (normally brown in absence of starch)
    d. To supply energy by respiration/to produce cellulose for cell wall

structure

2. Carbon dioxide + water → glucose + oxygen. Third mark for 'light energy' above arrow.
3. Magnesium is required for production of chlorophyll (no chlorophyll = brown). No chlorophyll = no photosynthesis so leaves will be withered.

Unit 6.4

LL C: oxygen concentration

1. **a.** 3.5 arbitrary units
    b. Light intensity is the limiting factor up to 6 arbitrary units. At this point, some other factor (temperature, for example) is at a value which is preventing further photosynthesis.

Unit 6.6

LL B: raise carbon dioxide concentration

1. **a.** Light intensity 10 arbitrary units, carbon dioxide concentration 0.15% at 30°C. Make sure that you give all of the units in your answer!
    b. Even at the same light intensity and temperature, increasing the carbon dioxide concentration from 0.04% to 0.15% increased the rate of photosynthesis by as much as 375%.
    c. Carbon dioxide concentration is the limiting factor under those sets of conditions

Unit 6.7

LL B: stomata

1. **a.** A – upper epidermis; B – palisade mesophyll; C – spongy mesophyll; D – guard cell; E – xylem vessel
    b. B
    c. E
    d. sucrose
    e. **i.** 0.9 mm   **ii.** 0.25 mm

Unit 6.8

LL **a.** chlorophyll   **b.** chloroplast

1. **a.** **i.** carbon dioxide   **ii.** oxygen
    b. diffusion
    c. **i.** This-stroy 19.5 g   water 33.0 g
        ii. 33.0 – 19.5 = 13.5 $\frac{13.5}{33.0} \times 100 = 59.1\%$
    d. reduces evaporation from leaf surface

Unit 6.9

LL Magnesium; nitrate; active transport

1. **a.** **i.** To allow measurement of the maximum (complete solution) and minimum (water) rate of growth of the wheat seedlings.
        ii. Air contains oxygen and oxygen is needed for aerobic respiration. This releases energy for active uptake of mineral ions by the root hair cells.
        iii. Magnesium is required to produce chlorophyll. No chlorophyll means very limited photosynthesis so very poor growth.
    b. nitrogen; phosphorus; potassium

Unit 7.1

LL C: carbohydrates

1. **a.** 70% = 55% + 15% (each segment represents 5%)
    b. From the top of the list: T; F; T; F; T; T; T; F; T; F; F; T; F; F; T; F

Unit 7.3

LL Obesity; diabetes

1. **a.** *y* axis energy requirement (kJ/day × 1000), *x* axis type of person
    b. age – teenage boy needs more energy than eight year old; gender – male IT worker needs more energy than female IT worker; activity – manual worker needs more energy than IT worker
    c. Female is lighter than a male, so less mass to move about

Unit 7.4

LL rickets

1. **a.** **i.** male   **ii.** female, aged 20–24
    b. **i.** as fat   **ii.** diabetes/arthritis/heart disease
    c. Provision of an unbalanced diet
    d. **i.** vitamin D   **ii.** calcium
        iii. Lack of growth/replacement of enzymes

Unit 7.5

LL C: lipase
1. a. With iodine solution: straw-brown; blue-black; blue-black; blue-black
   With Benedict's reagent: orange-red; blue; blue; blue
   b. Mouth (from salivary glands), small intestine (from pancreas)
   c. This is the optimum temperature for amylase activity
   d. In the stomach

Unit 7.6
LL Molar – crushing; incisor – biting; canine – killing/piercing
1. a. A – dentine   B – cement   C – crown
   b. vitamin C
2. a. Using a pH meter on a sample of saliva collected (e.g. by chewing a rubber band)
   b. pH affects the number of fillings
   c. Hypothesis supported; the increased pH shows a reduction in the number of fillings

Unit 7.7
LL saliva; amylase; hydrogencarbonate; alkaline
1. a. From top of diagram: epiglottis; entrance to trachea; contracted circular muscle; bolus of food; contracted circular muscle; relaxed circular muscle; stomach; pyloric sphincter
   b. Lubricate bolus/moisten food/add amylase/add alkaline hydrogencarbonate

Unit 7.8
LL D: villi
1. a. villus
   b. small intestine/ileum
   c. i. M – should be linked to lacteal (at centre of villus)
      ii. N – should be linked to surface epithelium (produces mucus from goblet cells)
   d. Large surface area increases rate of absorption, thin epithelium reduces distance for absorption, capillaries/lacteals remove absorbed products
   e. i. × 50   ii. 1.5 mm

Unit 8.1
LL A – sucrose; B – xylem; C – epidermis; D – phloem
1. a. A: phloem   B: xylem   C: epidermis
   b. i. B because this is xylem which transports water and water-soluble dyes such as eosin
      ii. Radioactive carbon dioxide is converted to radioactive carbohydrate by photosynthesis. The carbohydrate is transported, as sucrose, in the phloem. The phloem therefore shows up by fogging the photographic plate.

Unit 8.2
LL Support; photosynthesis; roots/root hairs; leaves/stomata
1. Osmosis; hairs; surface area; ions; magnesium; diffusion; active transport; support; solvent; photosynthesis
2. collect sample of leaves/weigh/allow to hang for 24 hours/reweigh/compare masses

Unit 8.3
LL False (water only)
1. a. Mean mass at start = 220.4 g. Mean mass after 24 h = 210.2 g
   Therefore mean loss of water = 220.4 − 210.2 = 10.2 g
   b. Mean volume of water at start = 100 cm³ = 100 g
   Mean volume of water after 24 h = 88 cm³ = 88 g
   Therefore mean uptake of water = 12 g
   c. Water uptake is driven by water loss from the stomata/leaves. Water lost 'pulls' a stream of water through the plant – this is replaced by water uptake at the roots.
   d. Some of the water absorbed by the roots is used for support or in photosynthesis, so the masses are not exactly the same.

Unit 8.4
LL aphids
1. a. A: xylem on top, phloem below   B: xylem on top, phloem below
   b. i. leaf – arrow towards stem; stem arrow at both ends of line; root – arrow down
      ii. glucose / sugars

Unit 9.1
LL Aorta – main artery in the body; renal artery – blood input to kidney; hepatic vein – blood output from liver; pulmonary artery – from heart to lungs
1. a. i. pulmonary vein
      ii. A has less oxygen/more carbon dioxide/is at higher pressure
   b. E has more urea/more sodium/is at higher pressure
   c. Should be guideline to vessel just below chamber C

Unit 9.2
LL 1 – true; 2 – false
1. a. i. left ventricle   ii. thicker muscular walls
   b. pacemaker; 72
2. a. double
   b. Blood pressure falls as blood passes through the gills, and cannot be raised again before blood reaches body tissues
   c. kidneys
   d. Blood at low pressure can flow more easily through the wider veins
   e. pulmonary arteries; tissue fluid/plasma

Unit 9.3
LL Increase in heart rate and increase in stroke volume
1. a. Change the depth of heartbeat (stroke volume), i.e. volume of blood pumped with each heartbeat
   b. i. X – cuspid valve, pressure in ventricle exceeds pressure in atrium so valve closes to prevent backflow
      Y – semilunar valve closes, as pressure in left ventricle falls below pressure in aorta, to prevent backflow of blood into heart
      ii. in the veins
      iii. Maintain one way flow of blood at lower pressure in the veins
   c. Blood flow to lungs is reduced so blood does not oxygenate well, and so blood (which shows up in the lips) is not as red as it normally would be

Unit 9.4
LL Pressure is lower in a vein, so no excess loss of blood
1. a. i. aorta   ii. arterioles
   b. i. capillaries
      ii. large cross-sectional area/low speed of travel of blood

Unit 9.5
LL C: low vitamin D concentration
1. a. i. Exercise increases blood flow to heart muscles and skin, but reduces blood flow to gut and kidneys. Flow to brain does not change.
      ii. Blood delivers more oxygen and glucose for respiration needed to release the energy required for muscle contraction.
   b. i. Less oxygen is delivered to working heart muscle, so less energy is available and muscle stops working
      ii. obesity/high fat consumption/high salt consumption

Unit 9.6
1. $5\,000\,000 = 5 \times 10^6$
2. a. Volume of blood $= 5 \times 10^3 \times 10^3 = 5 \times 10^6$
   b. Therefore total number of RBC in circulation $= 5 \times 10^6 \times 5 \times 10^6$
      $= 25 \times 10^{12} = 2.5 \times 10^{13}$
   c. Number replaced every day $= 2.5 \times \dfrac{10^{13}}{10^2} = 2.5 \times 10^{11}$

Unit 9.7
LL 1 – false; 2 – true; 3 – true
1. a. i. $100 - 45 = 55\%$
      ii. ions/glucose/amino acids/hormones
      iii. red blood cell – transport of oxygen; phagocyte – engulfing invading microbes; lymphocyte – antibody production; platelet – part of clotting process
   b. Severe breathlessness/tiredness/inability to train hard
   c. They will have an increased number of red blood cells, so their blood will be able to supply an increased amount of oxygen to the muscles, thus improving their performance.
   d. Testosterone (or some other steroid) – used because it increases growth of muscle tissue; anabolic steroid/muscle building; stimulants such as amphetamine/more powerful muscle contractions

Unit 10.1

LL D: a pathogen

1. a. high temperature/vomiting/diarrhoea
    b. not washing hands when preparing food for child/not using clean utensils and crockery/feeding with infected food
    c. Always wash hands when preparing food for child/cook food thoroughly and at the correct temperature
2. Rickets/scurvy; cystic fibrosis/sickle cell anaemia; dementia/heart disease/cancer; lung cancer/CHD/diabetes type II
3. in water/on surfaces touched by infected person/as particles in coughs and sneezes

Unit 10.2

LL B: clotting of blood

1. pathogen – a disease-causing organism; transmissible disease – condition in which the pathogen can be passed from one host to another; antigen – a substance which triggers the immune response; skin and nasal hairs – external barriers to infection; active immunity – defence against a pathogen by antibody production in the body; passive immunity – short-term defence by provision of antibodies from another individual; phagocyte – white blood cell that engulfs pathogens; lymphocyte – cell which produces antibodies
2. a. A chemical or cell which provokes the body's immune system to produce appropriate antibodies
    b. Response is faster/greater/lasts for longer

Unit 10.3

LL memory cells

1. a. from left to right: lymphocyte; antibody; pathogen; antigen
    b. The antibodies may penetrate the pathogen and allow it to burst as water enters/phagocytes can be alerted by the presence of the antibody, and can then engulf and digest the pathogen
    c. vaccination

Unit 10.4

LL B: vaccine

1. a. Defence against a pathogen by the production of antibodies in the body
    b. Antibodies are from another individual/the response does not last as long/no memory cells are produced.
    c. active; passive; passive; passive; active
2. a. vector
    b. To avoid risk of causing disease

Unit 10.5

LL A: an antibiotic

1. a. Food source column: fish; milk products; fresh meat; vegetables. Number of reported outbreaks column: 20; 45; 5
    b. At refrigeration temperatures, bacteria which might be present in the food cannot multiply, so cannot produce toxins which cause food poisoning

Unit 10.6

LL colon; rectum; anus

1. a. i. colon   ii. rectum
        iii. small extension of caecum on LH side of diagram
    b. i. cholera
        ii. diarrhoea – colon is unable to reabsorb water due to a salt imbalance
    c. The pathogen (bacterium) is transmitted in faeces/clean water is treated to kill bacteria

Unit 11.1

LL Bronchioles; bronchi; trachea

1. a. M – trachea;   N – bronchus;   O – bronchiole
    b. label lines to intercostal (between the rib) muscles and the diaphragm (below lungs)
    c. growth/cell division/active transport/heat generation
    d. carbon dioxide/water vapour

Unit 11.2

LL alveoli/air sacs; diffusion; carbon dioxide

1. a. Oxygen from alveolus to blood, and carbon dioxide from blood to alveolus.
    b. Large surface area/moist lining/very thin walls/closeness to capillary system
    c. pulmonary artery
2. a. emphysema or COPD.
    b. Reduction of surface area available for gas exchange as walls of air sacs are destroyed.
3. glucose + oxygen → carbon dioxide + water + energy

Unit 11.3

LL 1 – false; 2 – false

1. a. lung
    b. Label a line drawn across the thorax below the lung
    c. external intercostal muscles
    d. Intercostal muscles relax so front of thorax falls. Diaphragm relaxes so bottom of the thorax rises. Lung volume falls, so air is pushed out (exhaled).

Unit 11.4

LL B: 1600 cm³

1. a. $\frac{2500}{5} = 500$ cm³ per breath $\frac{8000}{5} = 1600$ cm³ per breath
        i.e. exercise has increased the depth of breathing.
    b. i. carbon dioxide   ii. diffusion

Unit 12.1

LL C: it is broken down to release energy

1. a. i. aerobic respiration
        ii. Towards the glass tube with the fruits in it
        iii. The fruits use up oxygen, and the carbon dioxide they release is absorbed by the soda lime. Therefore the volume of gas inside the tube falls.
        iv. $\frac{40}{5} = 8.$ $8 \times 0.25 = 2$ cm. Therefore the marker drop will be at 3.25 on the scale (i.e. current position is 5.25)
        v. Suitable control would be the tube set up exactly the same but without the tomato fruits
    b. Nitrogen gas does not allow respiration so that the fruits will not over-ripen and become 'spoiled'.

Unit 12.2

1. a. independent – type of fruit; dependent – rate of respiration; fixed – temperature/mass of fruit/volume of air available
    b. Type of fruit; Experiment 1; Experiment 2; Experiment 3; Mean rate of respiration of fruit (mm³ used per min per g of fruit).
    c. Type of fruit on x axis, rate of respiration on y axis, bar chart, points plotted correctly.

Unit 12.4

LL C: lactic acid

1. a. i. $C_6H_{12}O_6 + 6O_2 \rightarrow 6CO_2 + 6H_2O$ + energy
        ii. Respiration is catalysed by enzymes, which are affected by temperature
    b. i. Pie chart B – most of the energy must be supplied by aerobic respiration as the athlete could not continue to run if anaerobic respiration was the energy supplier (much less efficient, and lactate is toxic).
        ii. Performance is reduced as the lactic acid stops impulses reaching the muscle cells.
        iii. The lactic acid is removed by diffusing into the blood
    c. The extra oxygen required to remove lactic acid accumulated during anaerobic exercise.

Unit 13.1

LL D: excretion

1. a. The removal of toxins, the waste products of metabolism and substances in excess of requirements
    b. From top, and reading right to left: living cells; respiration; lungs; urea; liver; kidneys; absorption in gut; kidneys

c. i. deamination (production of urea from excess amino acids)/ storage of glycogen/removal of toxins such as alcohol

ii. A – bile duct – bile; B – pancreatic duct – enzymes including amylase and protease; C – small intestine – food; D – hepatic portal vein – dissolved foods; E – hepatic artery – oxygenated blood; F – hepatic vein – deoxygenated blood

Unit 13.2

LL   D: excretory

1. a. renal artery
   b. glomerulus
   c. The membrane is selective – pores are too small to allow passage of blood cells
   d. Mitochondria to supply energy for active transport/microvilli to provide increased surface area for absorption
   e. ureter

Unit 13.3

LL   true

1. a. alkali/ammonia
   b. Optimum temperature for the activity of the enzyme urease
   c. i. protein and glucose
      ii. They are reabsorbed in the first coiled tubule of the nephron
   d. As a control, to show no result for these tests if only water is available to the urease

Unit 14.1

LL   myelin; insulator; impulse/action potential

1. From the top of the table: A; C; E/F; E; D; B

Unit 14.2

LL   rapid/involuntary/positive survival value

1. a. i. nose
      ii. They always have a survival value, e.g. blinking clears the eye of particles of dust
   b. i. 1 – receptor   2 – sensory neurone   3 – white matter
      4 – grey matter   5 – association neurone   6 – synapse
      7 – motor neurone
      ii. muscles – contract; glands – secrete (e.g. a hormone)

Unit 14.3

LL   neurone; dendrites; axon

1. a. i. A molecule, produced in the synaptic vesicles and released across the synaptic cleft where it can bind with receptors on the postsynaptic membrane
      ii. A minute gap at a junction between adjacent neurones
   b. Operates as a valve – ensures impulses only travel in one direction

Unit 14.4

LL   B: stimulus

1. a. A eye – to sight the ball; B nose – to smell; C touch receptor in skin – to feel the racquet in his hand; D semicircular canals in ear – detects position
   b. An electrical impulse, which travels as a wave of ion movements along the sensory neurones

Unit 14.5

LL   B: rectum

1. a. From the top of the table: C; F; B; A; E; D.
   b. i. stimulus is bright light; receptor is retina; co-ordinator is central nervous system; effector is iris; response is reduce diameter of pupil
      ii. Prevents bright light from damaging the retina

Unit 14.6

LL   C: pancreas

1. a. Hormone: a chemical, produced by an endocrine organ, released into the bloodstream where it brings about a response at a target organ
   Target organ: an organ which brings about a response to stimulation by a specific hormone
   b. Hormones: slower/longer-lasting/more general than nervous control

2. Across:
   1. testosterone
   4. insulin
   5. messenger
   6. adrenaline

   Down:
   2. endocrine
   3. glucagon

Unit 14.7

LL   Homeostasis; negative

   a. line graph
   b. time taken to digest carbohydrates/absorb glucose
   c. i. insulin is secreted which increases uptake (and storage as glycogen) by liver and muscle
      ii. in negative feedback a change (rise in blood glucose) causes a process which reduces the effects of the change (release of insulin)
   d. line graph
   e. i. adrenaline is released/increases conversion of glycogen to glucose
      ii. increased heart rate/redistribution of blood from skin to muscles/pupils dilate/breathing rate increases/shallow depth of breathing

Unit 14.8

LL   A: shivering

1. a. A – sweat duct/pore;   B – dermis;   C – branch of vein
   b. They act as insulation – to retain heat within the body
   c. Optimum temperature for enzymes/cell membranes do not break down/solutes remain dissolved in plasma

Unit 14.9

LL   AUXIN; GRAVITROPISM; PHOTOTROPISM

1. a. i. Auxin has moved downwards and to the non-illuminated side of the shoot.
      ii. Auxin moves to non-illuminated side – causes enlargement of cells on this side – shoot therefore bends towards the light.
      iii. response – (positive) phototropism; benefit – moves leaves into the optimum position for photosynthesis
   b. Coordinating formation of fruit for easier harvesting;
      Acting as a weedkiller in growing crops

Unit 15.1

LL   C

1. a. bar chart
   b. $\frac{4}{200} \times 100 = 2\%$
   c. antibiotics are not effective against viral diseases
      Presence of antibiotics may select antibiotic-resistant bacteria

Unit 15.2

LL   a. lungs b. nicotine

1. a. i. Effect of age on the likelihood of COPD
      ii. chronic obstructive pulmonary disorder
      iii. No – there is no information about smoking, only about the age of sufferers from COPD
   b. Vital capacity would fall. This is because smoking damages the alveoli so that they become less elastic. As a result they cannot stretch so the vital capacity is reduced.

Unit 15.3

LL   a. iron/ferrous ion
   b. They must be able to pass through very narrow capillaries.

1. If carbon monoxide combines with the haemoglobin, the red blood cells cannot carry so much oxygen. The developing fetus requires oxygen from its mother's blood, so will suffer if the mother has less oxygen in her red cells.

2. a. Smoker of 20 cigarettes per day has a risk factor of 2.3, a non-smoker has a risk factor of 0.1. Therefore a smoker is about 23 times more likely to die from lung cancer.
   b. Smoker of 1–14 cigarettes a day is 13 times more likely to die of lung cancer than a non-smoker.

Unit 16.1

LL B: The offspring are genetically identical

1. **a.** mitosis in the second box in the asexual diagram, meiosis in the second box in the sexual diagram.
    b. for asexual nn and nn; for sexual n and n
    c. Advantage: rapid/progeny well adapted to same environment as parents
    Disadvantage: no variation possible, so great risk if 'unknown' infection attacks population

Unit 16.2

LL C: anther

1. **a.** Transfer of pollen from anther to the stigma.
    b. W – anther; X – ovary; Y – stigma; Z – petal
2. Petals: small and dull-coloured; large and brightly coloured; attraction of insects
    Anthers: hang out into the wind; kept deep inside flower; anthers can release pollen into the wind
    Pollen: very light; heavy and produced in smaller quantities; light pollen can float in the wind
    Stigma: branched; deep within flower, strong; branched to catch wind-blown pollen/strong to avoid damage from visiting insect

Unit 16.4

LL D: The transfer of pollen from stamen to stigma of a flower.

1. **a.** **i.** Mark P on tip of stigma
        ii. stigma
    b. **i.** Show entry via the micropyle
        ii. Male nucleus fuses with female nucleus to form a diploid zygote. Permits variation by random combination of genetic material from parent plants.

Unit 16.5

LL embryo; starch; testa

1. **a.** From the top of the column: E; C; B; A; D; F
    b. Show tube growth down style and entry to ovule via the micropyle
    c. **i.** plumule and radicle   **ii.** starch
        iii. iodine solution has changed from straw-brown to blue-black

Unit 16.7

LL height/body mass/length of index finger

1. **a.** 2; 10; 22; 15; 1
    b. number of seeds in pod on x axis, number of pods on y axis, bars should be touching
    c. 6
    d. $\frac{22}{50} \times 100 = 44\%$

Unit 16.8

LL D: They contain the haploid number of chromosomes

1. **a.** A: sperm duct/vas deferens; B: urethra; C: testis; D: scrotal sac/scrotum; E: penis; F: prostate gland
    b. i.–v. in order; C; F; C; B; A
    c. E – A – D – B – F – C

Unit 16.9

LL A: uterus

1. **a.** B; **b.** A; **c.** F; **d.** C; **e.** D

Unit 16.10

LL IVF = in vitro fertilisation; AI = artificial insemination

1. **a.** LH and oestrogen would combine to increase the possibility of ovulation
    b. FSH increases the production of ova
    c. Feedback inhibition of LH and FSH

Unit 16.11

LL A: gestation period

1. **a.** **i.** amniotic cavity – contains amniotic fluid which acts as a shock absorber; uterus wall – muscular and so is protection against physical damage
        ii. from end of umbilical cord to wall of uterus

    b. glucose: from mother to fetus; haemoglobin: no movement across placenta; nicotine: from mother to fetus; amino acids – from mother to fetus; carbon dioxide: from fetus to mother; alcohol: from mother to fetus; urea: from fetus to mother

Unit 16.12

LL puberty; sex hormones; secondary sexual

1. **a.** **i.** pituitary gland
        ii. testosterone
    b. breasts – for production of milk; hips – to accommodate the growing fetus in the uterus
    c. menopause

Unit 16.13

LL C: white blood cells

1. **a.** **i.** bacterium   **ii.** painful urination   **iii.** condom
    b. **i.** Reduces the production of defensive white blood cells
        ii. AIDS is viral, and so is not affected by antibiotics, which can control the bacterium causing gonorrhoea.

Unit 17.1

LL D: gene

1. **a.** GCCTATG
    b. **i.** messenger RNA   **ii.** ribosome
    c. amino acid
    d. **i.** protein
        ii. haemoglobin; antibodies; can recognise and bind to a neurotransmitter; enzyme which breaks down fats to fatty acids and glycerol; keratin

Unit 17.2

LL Deoxyribonucleic acid. The substance is acidic/found in the nucleus (at least originally)/contains the sugar deoxyribose.

1. From the top of the table: TRUE; FALSE; TRUE; TRUE; TRUE; TRUE; FALSE; TRUE; TRUE; TRUE
2. C
3. RNA single stranded, DNA double stranded; RNA has the base uracil instead of thymine.

Unit 17.3

LL C

1. **a.** nucleus **b.** white **c.** B **d.** identical twins
    e. **i.** identify which individuals are most closely related and do not let them breed with one another
        ii. examine DNA fingerprint and see how many different fingerprints (perhaps different species) there are in the new habitat
    f. 64

Unit 17.4

LL C: Two cells with 46 chromosomes each.

1. **a.** Male nerve cell: 46 XY; female white blood cell 46 XX; sperm cell: 23 X or Y; egg cell: 23 X; red blood cell 0 none
    b. mitosis
2. **a.** 4   **b.** mitosis
    c. bone marrow/liver/skin/apical meristem of plant

Unit 17.5

LL B: red blood cell (no chromosomes) and sperm cell (haploid)

1. **a.** One large and one small in each of the daughter cells
    b. **i.** ovary/testis   **ii.** anther/ovule
    c. To reduce the number of chromosomes to half so that at fertilisation the 'normal' (diploid) number is restored

Unit 17.6

LL A: have brown eyes but different genotypes

1. gene; meiosis; haploid; fertilisation; diploid; recessive; heterozygous
2. genotype – the set of alleles present in an organism; homozygous – having two identical alleles; dominant – an allele that is always expressed if it is present; heterozygous – having two alternative alleles; recessive – allele that is only expressed in a homozygous individual; chromosome – a thread-like structure of DNA…; allele – one alternative form of a gene; phenotype – the observable features of an organism

Answers

Unit 17.7
LL C: the child could receive the recessive allele from each parent
1. **a.** **i.** gender/eye colour/blood group
   ii. an alternative form of a gene
   iii. Show a number of genes lined up along a thread-like chromosome
   b. **i.** 9 **ii.** could be Rr or RR **iii.** $\frac{3}{4}$ or 75%

Unit 17.8
LL A: AO and BO
1. **a.** **i.** Andrew and John
   ii. blood group – a discontinuous variation, so affected by genes only
   iii. nutrition – David might eat more high-calorie foods, or take less exercise
   b. codominance

Unit 17.9
LL D: a girl who is a carrier for colour blindness
1. **a.** 2 has two X chromosomes, 3 has two X chromosomes 5 has one X and one Y chromosome
   b. 2 could have H and h, 3 could have h and h, 5 could be h
   c. female – female – female – male – male
   d. **i.** X^hX^H **ii.** Correct Punnett square **iii.** 25%

Unit 18.1
LL phenotype; genotype; environment
1. continuous variation – a form of variation with many intermediate forms between the extremes; gene – a section of DNA responsible for an inherited characteristic; discontinuous variation – a form of variation with clear-cut differences between groups; phenotype – the observable features of an organism; height in humans – one example of continuous variation; environment – this factor, in addition to genotype, can affect phenotype; nutrients – one possible form of environmental influence on variation; blood group – one example of discontinuous variation.
2. **a.** **i.** Organisms with so many common features that they may interbreed and produce fertile offspring.
   ii. A change in the type or quantity of DNA in an individual.
   iii. A section of DNA responsible for coding for a single protein/characteristic.
   b. radiation; carcinogenic chemicals such as tar in cigarette smoke

Unit 18.2
LL Discontinuous caused by genes only, continuous caused by genes plus effects of the environment.
1. **a.** 1 – 2 – 4 – 6 – 10 – 5 – 3 – 2 – 1
   b. mass category on x axis, number in group on y axis, bars should be touching
   c. Continuous variation
   d. A result of a combination of genotype and effects of the environment.

Unit 18.3
LL Adaptation; genotype
1. **a.** Artificial; artificial; natural; natural; natural
   b. **i.** By selecting individual animals with a high milk yield, breeding them, then selecting from their offspring cows that have a high milk yield, then breeding them, and so on.
   ii. resistance to disease/ability to withstand difficult environmental conditions such as low temperatures

Unit 18.4
LL B: is well camouflaged from its natural predators
1. **a.** B – E – C – A – D
   b. From left to right: heron – feeds by spearing fish and frogs; hawk – captures Florida rabbits and other mammals; spoonbill – filters algae and other small organisms from the water; finch – feeds on nuts and other hard fruits; warbler – feeds by catching small insects

Unit 18.5
LL species; artificial selection/selective breeding
1. **a.** Brussels sprouts – bud; broccoli – flower
   b. **i.** They have been produced by mitosis, so there is very little possibility of genetic variation.

ii. nitrate – the ion needed for protein synthesis (growth); plants in closed environment – temperature and humidity can be controlled so that cuttings do not dry out

Unit 19.1
LL B: solar energy from the Sun
1. **a.** **i.** the Sun **ii.** feeding
   iii. some is reflected/the wrong wavelength/does not fall on leaves
   iv. respiration – energy is lost here as heat
   b. **i.** A: $\frac{15000}{90000} \times \frac{100}{1} = 16.6\%$ B: $\frac{2000}{15000} \times \frac{100}{1} = 13.3\%$
   ii. Each stage in the food chain allows a loss of energy as heat. Fewer steps, as in eating a vegetarian diet, mean that more energy is transferred as heat loss.

Unit 19.2
LL mass of individuals; number of individuals
1. food chain – the transfer of energy from one organism to the next, beginning with a producer; food web – a network of interconnected food chains; producer – an organism that makes its own organic nutrients, usually through photosynthesis; consumer – an organism that gets its energy by feeding on other organisms; herbivore – an animal that gets its energy from eating plants; carnivore – an animal that gets its energy by eating other animals; decomposer – an organism that gets its energy from dead or waste material
2. Pyramid should have broad base, of algae, then gradually narrowing through water fleas, smelt and to the pointed peak at kingfisher

Unit 19.3
LL A: kilojoules
1. **a.** There are fewer steps in the food chain leading to grains and seeds, so fewer opportunities for loss of energy.
   b. Less of the food supplied to the sheep is used to generate heat to maintain their body temperature, so more can be used for protein synthesis/growth.

Unit 19.4
LL photosynthesis; respiration
1. **a.** From left to right: photosynthesis; respiration; feeding; decay
   b. It would raise the carbon dioxide concentration in the air

Unit 19.5
LL Nitrate; nitrogen gas; denitrifying bacteria
1. **a.** **i.** B – feeding E – denitrification
   ii. decomposition/decay by bacteria and fungi
   b. **i.** ammonium concentration would rise/nitrite and nitrate levels would fall/fewer dead leaves would be decomposed
   ii. ticks in few scavenging insects/regular turning of the heap to add air

Unit 19.6
LL lag – exponential – stationary – decline
1. **a.** higher death rate/less food/lower birth rate/emigration
   b. vaccination/immunisation programmes; use of antibiotics; improved surgical techniques; fewer deaths at childbirth
   c. use of antibiotics/antiseptics; thorough cooking to reduce food-poisoning bacteria

Unit 19.7
LL prokaryotes; nucleus; cell wall; binary fission
1. **a.** time on x axis, number of bacteria on y axis
   b. sugar – energy from respiration; amino acids – protein synthesis; sterile – prevent competition from other bacterial species
   c. show steepest part of curve
   d. shortage of oxygen/nutrients, e.g. glucose or amino acids

Unit 20.1
LL D: milk
1. **a.** **i.** beans **ii.** rice **iii.** vitamins and minerals
   b. drought/loss of nutrients from soil/displacement of populations by war

Unit 20.2
LL nesting sites; soil
1. loss of habitat for animals/possible soil erosion/changes to water cycle/possible loss of valuable medicinal plants

Answers

2. a. i.   Marsh has been drained/hedges have been removed/there are more buildings in 2003
        ii. Marsh animals would be reduced in number, e.g. frogs need water in which to lay their eggs; hedge removal would mean fewer nesting sites for birds; hedge removal would eliminate certain food plants for insects such as butterflies
    b. Loss of nesting sites/soil erosion/loss of food plants for some species/less removal of carbon dioxide from the atmosphere/ disturbance of water cycle

Unit 20.3
LL   A: sulfur dioxide and nitrogen oxides
1. a. The gases form a layer around the Earth which allows radiation in but does not allow thermal radiation out – the surface of the Earth therefore becomes warmer
    b. 1. These renewable energy resources do not produce greenhouse gases
        2. Insulation means less heat loss so less combustion of fossil fuels for heating
        3. Reforestation increases the number of plants which can remove carbon dioxide from the atmosphere during photosynthesis
2. Removal of habitat for road construction/disturbance of wildlife by noise and presence of humans/pollution from vehicle exhausts

Unit 20.4
LL   A: are washed into rivers and pollute the water
1. a. C – E – B – D – A
    b. Run-off of fertilisers from nearby farmland
    c. Bacteria respire aerobically, using dead plants as food source / aerobic respiration by bacteria reduces oxygen concentration in the water / fish and larger invertebrates die as they are short of oxygen

Unit 20.5
LL   carbon dioxide; methane
1. a. carbon dioxide + water $\longrightarrow$ glucose + oxygen: this process is driven by light energy
    b. The biocoil must be transparent to allow light to penetrate to the algae
    c. The algae are removed to use as a fuel – they must be replaced quickly if the process is to be economical

Unit 20.6
LL   C: legumes
1. a. More shoals of fish are located, and more are caught by the fine mesh. Few fish escape to breed, so the population decreases. Loss of one species will affect the numbers of other species in the food web for this habitat.
    b. Increase size of mesh/restrict areas in which fishing can take place/ restrict times of year in which fishing can take place/limit the size of the catch for each fishing vessel
2. a. Biuret test – solution containing protein turns solution from blue to purple/mauve.
    b. Uptake of calcium needed for strong growth of teeth and bones/ avoid rickets.

Unit 20.7
LL   Habitat; reproduce
1. Management of the environment to maintain biodiversity
2. a. i.   Environmental factor: removal of bamboo forests – bamboo shoots are the basic food of the giant panda
             Biological factor: pandas reproduce very slowly – number of births does not replace number of dying pandas, so population falls
        ii. Saving the panda (a very attractive species which many people will help to conserve) also protects other species in the same habitat
    b. i.   To find the population size at the start of the management plan
        ii. Many examples possible, e.g. butterflies – with nets, beetles – with pitfall traps, plants – with quadrats

Unit 20.8
LL   biodiversity; humans
1. a. A process which does not affect the environment for future generations
    b. Less competition for light/for nutrients/for water
    c. Limited food variety for animals/any pest or disease can affect all of the plants
    d. Any of them might be a benefit. Best might be fast growth (so product is available quickly), resistance to disease (so few plants are lost to disease) and good growth on poor soil (so few fertilisers are necessary).

Unit 20.9
LL   aluminum; recycled
1. a. i. photosynthesis   ii. diffusion   iii. it is raised
    b. i.   They are easier to decompose/they are unlikely to harm wildlife which might consume them.
        ii. printing newspapers/as packaging/as toilet paper/as paper towels

Unit 21.1
LL   D: plasmid
1. a. From the top of the table: F; F; T; T; F; T; T; T; T; T; T; F
    b. Typical bacterium is one millionth of a metre wide/bacteria are larger than viruses/many bacteria are not harmful, they are useful/ bacteria do not have a nucleus – they have 'naked' DNA

Unit 21.2
LL   pectinase
1. a. from the top: milk containing lactose   lactase   lactose-free milk
    b. Immobilisation – fixed onto an inert substance
        Importance – allows re-use of enzyme/provides product free of enzyme

Unit 21.3
LL   cellulose
1. a. $\frac{1000}{40} = 25$
        $25 \times 100 = 2500 \text{ cm}^3$
    b. i.   Pectinase is specific to breakdown of pectin. Amylase is a starch-digesting enzyme.
        ii. The higher temperature has increased enzyme activity, so more clear extract produced.
        iii. Any suitable example, e.g. protease/meat-softening lipase/ biscuit production (smoothing chocolate).

Unit 21.4
LL   B: fungi
1. a. (6–)7 days: this represents the maximum yield of penicillin – any time longer produces less penicillin and would be expensive in terms of energy and raw materials
    b. Some bacteria in the population have a natural resistance – the non-resistant bacteria are killed by the antibiotic – the resistant bacteria now multiply and produce a resistant population
    c. pectinase; protease; removes milk sugar from milk

Unit 21.5
LL   B: insulin
1. a. gene – a section of DNA coding for a protein; plasmid – a small circle of DNA in a bacterial cell; vector – a structure which can carry a gene into another cell; ligase – an enzyme that can splice one gene into another section of DNA; restriction – an enzyme that can cut a specific gene from a chromosome; sticky ends – pieces of single-stranded DNA left exposed after a gene is cut from a chromosome; fermenter – a vessel in which engineered bacteria can produce a valuable product under optimum conditions
    b. i.   insulin – control of blood sugar level
        ii. Factor 8 – one step in blood clotting
        iii. Pectinase – 'clears' fruit juices by breaking up clumps of plant tissue
        iv. Human growth hormone – can increase growth rate in humans of short stature
    c. the virus might not be completely inactivated, and thus may infect a patient with hepatitis

Unit 21.6

LL gene; DNA; DNA; chromosomes; nucleus

1. **a.** plasmid – D; restriction enzyme – E; gene probe – B; sequence of bases – C; clone – G; protein – A; bacterial cell – F

Language focus
Unit 22

Matching pairs

food chain – the transfer of energy from one organism to the next; producer – an organism that makes its own organic nutrients, usually using energy from sunlight; carnivore – an animal that gets its energy by eating other animals; trophic level – the position of an organism in a food chain; food web – a network of interconnected food chains; consumer – an organism that gets its energy by feeding on other organisms; herbivore – an animal that gets its energy by eating plants; decomposer – an organism that gets its energy from dead or waste organic material; community – all of the populations of different species in an ecosystem; population – a group of organisms of one species, living in the same area at the same time; ecosystem – a unit made up of the community of organisms interacting with their non-living environment

Word scrambles

SEXUAL REPRODUCTION; GAMETES; ZYGOTE; FERTILISATION; PUBERTY; SEX HORMONES; TESTES; OVARIES; VAGINA; PENIS; CONCEPTION; COPULATION; EMBRYO; MENSTRUATION; GROWTH; DEVELOPMENT; PLACENTA; GESTATION PERIOD; UMBILICAL CORD; AMNIOTIC FLUID

DNA, fingerprints, and forensics crossword

Across:
2. electrophoresis
4. haemoglobin
5. DNA
6. nucleotide
8. identical
9. protein
11. three
13. amino acid
14. thymine
15. nucleus
17. adenine
18. enzyme

Down:
1. Crick
3. complementary
5. double helix
7. four
10. forensic
11. twins
12. Watson
16. gene

Gas exchange crossword

Across:
1. capillaries
4. mucus
5. nitrogen
6. bronchioles
10. surface area
11. diaphragm
14. airsac
15. oxygen
18. dioxide
19. larynx
20. gills
21. water

Down:
2. intercostal
3. lungs
7. trachea
8. bronchus
9. vapour
11. diffusion
12. alveolus
13. carbon
16. cilia
17. goblet

Exam-style questions
Unit 24

1. C   2. B   3. D   4. A   5. A
6. C   7. A   8. A   9. A
10. **i.** A   **ii.** B   **iii.** D
11. **a.** Correct position above and to the right of the stomach
    b. peristalsis
    c. From the top of the column: A – A – C – E – F
12. **a.** **i.** A: respiration; B: photosynthesis C: feeding D: respiration.
       ii. decay/decomposition – a process in which organisms secrete enzymes which break down complex organic compounds such as proteins into simpler compounds such as amino acids/ammonium nitrate
    b. **i.** In the compost heap respiration is taking place. This releases energy, some of which is lost as heat.
       ii. This allows oxygen to penetrate the compost – oxygen is needed for aerobic respiration
13. **a.** **i.** large surface area/close to blood supply/moist lining
       ii. Allows stretching during the inhalation/exhalation cycle
    b. Blood at A has more carbon dioxide and less oxygen than blood at B
    c. Makes lung tissue less elastic/breaks down walls of alveoli/inactivates cilia in airways/may trigger development of cancer cells
14. **a.** A – 3;   B – 4;   C – 2;   D – 1
    b. **i.** meiosis   **ii.** mitosis
    c. **i.** stem cell   **ii.** bone marrow
15. **a.** G = Pp   K = PP
    b. two (D and E)   **c.** 0 (0%)   **d.** 0.5 (50%)
16. **a.** **i.** apple tree – apple moth caterpillar – thrush – owl
       ii. sunlight
    b. **i.** pyramid of biomass
       ii. the position of an organism in a food chain
       iii. Energy is lost (respiration) at each trophic level so that less than 100% is transferred from one trophic level to the next. As much as 90% is lost at each transfer, so there can be very few transfers.
       iv. loss of habitat/breeding site; hunting; loss of food source/prey
       v. captive breeding; provision of nature reserve; ban on hunting
17. **a.** raises blood pressure (which can damage narrow capillaries)
    b. **i.** 0.2 – 2.5 g
       ii. $(0.2 + 0.9 + 2.0 + 2.5 + 0.7 + 0.5 + 1.3) = 8.1$ $8.1 - 6.0 = 2.1g$
    c. toast and butter (butter is derived from milk)

Practical biology

1. **a.** Add Benedict's Reagent/heat in boiling water bath/change from blue to orange-red is a positive test for a simple sugar.
   b. Can be given a numerical value.
   c. Independent variable – type of milk; fixed variables – volume of sample/volume of Benedict's Reagent added/temperature of heating; dependent variable – quantity of sugar detected; use a colorimeter; water would be a suitable control; repeats mean that any 'rogue' result does not distort the value of the real result.

You will find that the practical paper or the alternative to practical will be much more straightforward if you recognise certain standard pieces of equipment, and understand what they are used for.

Apparatus and materials

Safety equipment appropriate to the work being planned, but at least including eye protection such as safety spectacles or goggles.

3D image	Name and function	Diagram
	■ **Watch glass**: used for collection and evaporating liquids with no heat, and for immersing biological specimens in a liquid.	
	■ **Filter funnel**: used to separate solids from liquids, using a filter paper.	
	■ **Measuring cylinder**: used for measuring the volume of liquids.	
	■ **Thermometer**: used to measure temperature.	

The other very important measuring device in the laboratory is a balance (weighing machine).

3D image	Name and function	Diagram
	■ **Spatula**: used for handling solid chemicals; for example, when adding a solid to a liquid.	
	■ **Pipette**: used to measure and transfer small volumes of liquids.	
	■ **Stand, boss, and clamp**: used to support the apparatus in place. This reduces the risk of dangerous spills. This is not generally drawn. If the clamp is merely to support a piece of apparatus, it is usually represented by two crosses as shown.	
	■ **Bunsen burner**: used to heat the contents of other apparatus (e.g. a liquid in a test tube) or for **directly** heating solids.	HEAT
	■ **Tripod**: used to support apparatus above a Bunsen burner. **The Bunsen burner, tripod, and gauze are the most common way of heating materials in school science laboratories.**	
	■ **Gauze**: used to spread out the heat from a Bunsen burner and to support the apparatus on a tripod.	
	■ **Test tube and boiling tube**: used for heating solids and liquids. They are also used to hold chemicals while other substances are added and mixed. They need to be put safely in a test tube rack.	
	■ **Evaporating dish**: used to collect and evaporate liquids with or without heating.	
	■ **Beaker**: used for mixing solutions and for heating liquids.	

Table of hazard symbols

Symbol	Description	Examples	Symbol	Description	Examples
	Oxidising These substances provide oxygen which allows other materials to burn more fiercely.	Bleach, sodium chlorate, potassium nitrate		**Harmful** These substances are similar to toxic substances but less dangerous.	Dilute acids and alkalis
	Highly flammable These substances easily catch fire.	Ethanol, petrol, acetone		**Corrosive** These substances attack and destroy living tissues, including eyes and skin.	Concentrated acids and akalis
	Toxic These substances can cause death. They may have their effects when swallowed or breathed in or absorbed through the skin.	Mercury, copper sulfate		**Irritant** These substances are not corrosive but can cause reddening or blistering of the skin.	Ammonia, dilute acids and alkalis

Reagent	Use in biology
hydrogencarbonate indicator (bicarbonate indicator)	Detects changes in carbon dioxide concentration, for example in exhaled air following respiration
[X] iodine in potassium iodide solution (iodine solution)	Detection of starch
[X] Benedict's solution (or an alternative such as Fehling's)	Detection of a reducing sugar, such as glucose
[biuret] biuret reagent(s) (sodium or potassium hydroxide solution and copper sulfate solution)	Detection of protein
[flammable] ethanol/methylated spirit	For dissolving lipids in testing for the presence of lipids. Also used to remove chlorophyll from leaves during starch testing.
cobalt chloride paper	Detects changes in water content
pH indicator paper or Universal Indicator solution or pH probes	Detects changes in pH during reactions such as digestion of fats to fatty acids and glycerol
litmus paper	Qualitative detection of pH
glucose	Change in water potential of solutions
sodium chloride	Change in water potential of solutions
aluminium foil or black paper	Foil can be used as a heat reflector: black paper as a light absorber
a source of distilled or deionised water	Change in water potential of solutions. Also used in making up mineral nutrient solutions.
eosin/red ink	To follow the pathway of water absorbed by plants
limewater	A liquid absorbent for carbon dioxide, for example in exhaled air
[X] methylene blue	A stain for animal cells
[biuret] potassium hydroxide	Removes carbon dioxide from the atmosphere, for example during experiments on conditions for photosythesis
sodium hydrogencarbonate (sodium bicarbonate)	Very mild alkali: used for adjusting pH of solutions for enzyme activity
petroleum jelly (or similar)	Blocks pores such as stomata, and so prevents water loss